QUILT-LOVERS' FAVORITES™

FROM AMERICAN PATCHWORK & QUILTING®

Better Homes and Gardens® Creative Collection™
Des Moines, Iowa

VOLUME 3

Better Homes and Gardens®

QUILT-LOVERS' FAVORITES™

FROM AMERICAN PATCHWORK & QUILTING®

Director of Editorial Administration	MICHAEL L. MAINE
Editor-in-Chief	BEVERLY RIVERS
Executive Editor	HEIDI KAISAND
Art Director	MELISSA GANSEN BEAUCHAMP
Senior Editor	JENNIFER KELTNER
Editor	DIANE YANNEY
Graphic Designer	MARY-BETH MAJEWSKI
Editorial Assistant	MARY IRISH
Contributing Editor	SUE BAHR AND SANDRA NEFF
Contributing Graphic Designer	BARBARA J. GORDON
Contributing Copy Editors	DIANE DORO, ANGIE INGLE, AND JENNIFER SPEER RAMUNDT
Quilt Tester	LAURA BOEHNKE
Technical Editor	LILA SCOTT
Contributing Watercolor Illustrator	ANN WEISS
Contributing Technical Illustrator	CHRIS NEUBAUER GRAPHICS
Publisher	MAUREEN RUTH
Consumer Products Marketing Director	BEN JONES
Consumer Products Marketing Managers	KARRIE NELSON AND STEVE SWANSON
Business Director	CHRISTY LIGHT
Production Director	DOUGLAS M. JOHNSTON
Book Production Managers	PAM KVITNE
	MARJORIE J. SCHENKELBERG
Marketing Assistant	CHERYL ECKERT
Vice President Publishing Director	WILLIAM R. REED

CORPORATION

Chairman and CEO	WILLIAM T. KERR
Chairman of the Executive Committee	E.T. MEREDITH III

Meredith Publishing Group

President	STEPHEN M. LACY
Magazine Group President	JERRY KAPLAN
Creative Services	ELLEN DE LATHOUDER
Manufacturing	BRUCE HESTON
Consumer Marketing	KARLA JEFFRIES
Finance and Administration	MAX RUNCIMAN

Member   Crafts. Discover life's little pleasures.   Audit Bureau of Circulations Member

For book editorial questions, write:

Better Homes and Gardens Quilt-Lovers' Favorites • *1716 Locust St., GA 205, Des Moines, IA 50309-3023*

TREASURED QUILTS

Sharing favorite quilt patterns is a custom as old as quilting itself. This third volume of Quilt-Lovers' Favorites™ *continues the tradition by sharing 15 of the quilts most often requested by readers of* American Patchwork & Quilting® *magazine.*

Each of these quilts is accompanied by additional projects using creative adaptations of the originally featured blocks, units, or appliqué shapes. You'll find items for every room in the house, inventive ways to embellish a wardrobe, and heart-warming gift possibilities.

Full-size patterns, step-by-step instructions, and Quilter's Schoolhouse, a start-to-finish reference guide on quiltmaking, will help assure success for quilters of all skill levels. Optional size charts mean you can alter quilt dimensions quickly and easily, and a variety of color options will spark your imagination.

Take your time looking through this book. If you do, I'm sure you'll be inspired to make a special quilt so you can experience the joy of creating something both beautiful and useful.

Heidi Kaisand

Executive Editor, American Patchwork & Quilting®

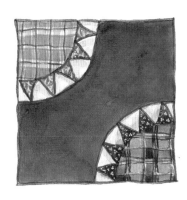

TABLE of CONTENTS

VINTAGE COLLECTION
Page **6**

ROUND ABOUT
Page **38**

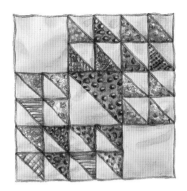

VINTAGE
COLLECTION

These are the quilts our grandmothers' mothers made, and their mothers before them.

From the variety of colors in "Triangles in a Triangle," to the mystifying geometrics of "King Solomon's Temple," to the casual perfection of "Checkerboard," these patterns have defined the art of quiltmaking over time.

Re-create these timeless designs in your own style. You'll make heirlooms with ageless appeal.

Triangles
IN A TRIANGLE

This familiar block was well established by the 1840s, when this antique quilt was made. Quilt historian Sara Rhodes Dillow favors its medley of materials, and echoed its color placement to set the same pattern in her vintage re-creation, shown on page 10.

Materials

3½ yards of dark blue print for large triangles

3¼ yards total of assorted light prints for
   small triangles

1¾ yards total of assorted medium and dark
   prints for small triangles

⅜ yard of solid red for inner border

2 yards of navy print for outer border and binding

4¼ yards of backing fabric

83×75" of quilt batting

Finished quilt top: 77×69"

Quantities specified for 44/45"-wide, 100% cotton fabrics. All measurements include a ¼" seam allowance. Sew with right sides together unless otherwise stated.

Cut the Fabrics

To make the best use of your fabrics, cut the pieces in the order that follows.

To make templates of the patterns, found on *Pattern Sheet 1*, follow the instructions in Quilter's Schoolhouse, which begins on *page 150*.

continued

To cut triangles quickly, start with strips. For Pattern A, first cut a 7¾"-wide strip. Then cut as many Pattern A triangles from the strip as you can. Repeat until you have a total of 60. In the same manner, for Pattern C, cut 3⅛"-wide strips.

From dark blue print, cut:
- 60 of Pattern A
- 4 *each* of patterns B and B reversed

From assorted light prints, cut:
- 376 of Pattern C
- 8 *each* of patterns D and D reversed

From assorted medium and dark prints, cut:
- 188 of Pattern C
- 4 *each* of patterns D and D reversed

From solid red, cut:
- 7—1½×42" strips for inner border

From navy print, cut:
- 8—6×42" strips for outer border
- 8—2½×42" binding strips

Assemble the Blocks

1. Referring to Diagram 1 for placement, sew two light print C triangles to a medium or dark print C triangle to make a subunit. Press the seam allowances toward the light print triangles. Repeat to make a total of 120 subunits. Reserve 60 subunits for Step 3.

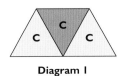

Diagram 1

2. Join a light print C triangle to the top edge of the 60 remaining Step 1 subunits as shown in Diagram 2.

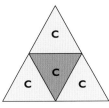

Diagram 2

3. Referring to Diagram 3, sew a medium or dark print C triangle to a light print C triangle to make a pair. Repeat to make 60 paired C triangles. Sew the 60 paired C triangles to the reserved Step 1 units. Press the seam allowances toward the light print triangles.

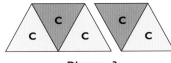

Diagram 3

4. Sew together the units from steps 2 and 3 to make a total of 60 pieced triangle blocks (see Diagram 4).

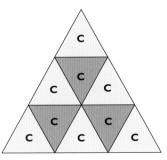

Diagram 4

5. Join the remaining light and dark print C triangles, dark print D triangles, and dark print D reversed triangles to make four of each half block shown in Diagram 5. Press the seam allowances toward the light print triangles.

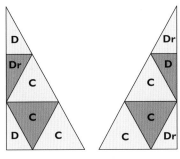

Diagram 5

Assemble the Quilt Center

1. Referring to the photograph *opposite* for placement, lay out the blocks and dark blue print A triangles in eight horizontal rows, alternating rows of eight dark blue print A triangles and seven pieced triangle blocks with rows of seven dark blue print A triangles and eight pieced triangle blocks. Then alternately add a dark blue print B triangle and a dark blue print B reversed triangle or pieced half block to the ends of each row.

2. Sew together the pieces in each row. Press the seam allowances in one direction, alternating the direction with each row. Then join the rows to make the quilt center. The pieced quilt center should measure 64½×56½", including the seam allowances.

Assemble and Add the Borders

The following border strip lengths are correct mathematically. Before cutting, measure the length and width of your pieced quilt center and adjust the length of your border strips accordingly.

1. Cut and piece the solid red 1½×42" strips to make the following:
   • 2—1½×64½" inner border strips
   • 2—1½×58½" inner border strips

2. Sew a long solid red inner border strip to the top and bottom edges of the pieced quilt center. Then join the short solid red inner border strips to the side edges of the pieced quilt center. Press the seam allowances toward the inner border.

3. Cut and piece the navy print 6×42" strips to make the following:
   • 2—6×69½" outer border strips
   • 2—6×66½" outer border strips

continued

4. Sew a short navy print outer border strip to the top and bottom edges of the pieced quilt center. Then join the long navy print outer border strips to the side edges of the quilt center to complete the quilt top. Press the seam allowances toward the outer border.

Complete the Quilt

1. Layer the quilt top, batting, and backing according to the instructions in Quilter's Schoolhouse, which begins on *page 150*. Quilt as desired.

2. Use the navy print 2½×42" strips to bind the quilt according to the instructions in Quilter's Schoolhouse.

Triangles in a Triangle Quilt
optional sizes

If you'd like to make this quilt in a size other than for a twin bed-size quilt, use the information *below*.

Alternate quilt sizes	Crib	Full/Queen	King
Number of blocks	18	102	136
Number of rows	5	12	13
Finished size	45×48"	85×97"	101×104"
Yardage requirements			
Dark blue print	1¼ yards	5⅞ yards	7⅝ yards
Assorted light prints	1⅛ yards	4⅛ yards	6¾ yards
Assorted medium and dark prints	⅝ yard	2⅝ yards	3½ yards
Solid red	¼ yard	½ yard	½ yard
Navy print	1⅜ yards	2½ yards	2¾ yards
Backing	2½ yards	7⅝ yards	9 yards
Batting	51×54"	91×103"	107×110"

optional colors

A border of pastel zoo animals is the basis for the color palette of this youthful version of "Triangles in a Triangle." Scraps of yellow, pink, blue, and green prints combine with triangles from the border fabric, fussy-cut to feature the critters, for the pieced triangles. A cream stripe for the large triangles balances the scrappy look.

TABLE RUNNER

The deep, rich hues of this table runner

create a palette reminiscent of Amish quilts.

The diamond pattern emerges when the

pieced triangle blocks are set end to end.

Materials

5/8 yard total of assorted dark prints for blocks

1 1/3 yards of black print for side triangles and
    outer border

1/4 yard of red print for inner border

1 yard of backing fabric

19×70" of quilt batting

Finished table runner top: 12¾×64"

continued

Cut the Fabrics

To make the best use of your fabrics, cut the pieces in the order that follows. This project uses "Triangles in a Triangle" patterns B and C on *Pattern Sheet 1.* To make templates of the patterns, follow the instructions in Quilter's Schoolhouse, which begins on *page 150.*

The outer border strips are cut the length of the fabric (parallel to the selvage). Extra length is added to allow for mitering the corners.

From assorted dark prints, cut:
- 72 of Pattern C

From black print, cut:
- 6 *each* of patterns B and B reversed
- 2—2½×45" outer border strips
- 4—2½×18" outer border strips

From red print, cut:
- 4—⅞×42" strips for inner border

Assemble the Table Runner Center

1. Referring to the Assemble the Blocks instructions on *page 10,* use nine dark print C triangles to make one pieced triangle block (see Diagram 4 on *page 11*). Make a total of eight pieced triangle blocks.

2. Sew a black print B triangle and a black print B reversed triangle to six of the pieced triangle blocks (see Block Assembly Diagram) to make framed triangle blocks. Each framed triangle block should now measure 8½×7½", including the seam allowances.

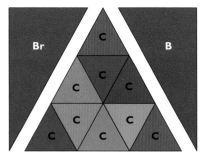

Block Assembly Diagram

3. Referring to the photograph *right* for placement, sew the framed triangle blocks together in a row. Press the seam allowances in one direction. Add a pieced triangle block to each end of the row to make the table runner center; press.

Add the Borders

1. Cut and piece the red print ⅞×42" strips to make the following:
   - 2—⅞×45" inner border strips
   - 4—⅞×18" inner border strips

2. Aligning long edges, sew together a red print ⅞×45" inner border strip and a black print 2½×45" outer border strip to make a pieced long border unit. Repeat to make a second pieced long border unit.

3. Aligning long edges, sew together the red print ⅞×18" inner border strips and the black print 2½×18" outer border strips to make a total of four pieced short border units.

4. With midpoints aligned, sew the long border units to the long edges of the pieced table runner center and the short border units to the angled edges of the pieced table runner center, beginning and ending the seams ¼" from the corners.

5. Miter the border corners. For information on mitering corners, see the instructions in Quilter's Schoolhouse, which begins on *page 150.* Press all seam allowances toward the outer border.

Complete the Table Runner

1. With right sides together, sew together the pieced table runner top, batting, and backing, leaving an opening along one long edge for turning. Trim the batting and backing even with the table runner top. Turn the table runner right side out and whipstitch the opening closed.

2. Quilt as desired.

RACE CAR QUILT

*For a themed quilt, set the large triangles
end to end, alternating a favorite print with
a coordinating solid. Here, the pieced
sashing sets the stage for the outer border.*

Materials

2¼ yards of solid black for blocks and binding

1¾ yards of red race car print for blocks

⅛ yard *each* of solid red, yellow, green, and blue
for inner border

1⅞ yards of black-and-white flag print for
outer border

3½ yards of backing fabric

69×63" of quilt batting

Finished quilt top: 63×57"

Cut the Fabrics

To make the best use of your fabrics, cut the pieces
in the order that follows. This project uses "Triangles
in a Triangle" patterns A and B on *Pattern Sheet 1*.
To make templates of the patterns, follow the
instructions in Quilter's Schoolhouse, which begins
on *page 150*.

The border strips are cut the length of the fabric
(parallel to the selvage).

From solid black, cut:
- 6—2½×42" binding strips
- 33 of Pattern A
- 3 *each* of patterns B and B reversed

From red race car print, cut:
- 33 of Pattern A
- 3 *each* of patterns B and B reversed

From *each* solid red, yellow, green, and blue, cut:
- 7—2×9" strips

From black-and-white flag print, cut:
- 2—6½×63½" outer border strips
- 2—6½×45½" outer border strips

Assemble the Quilt Center

1. Referring to the photograph on *page 16* for
   placement, lay out red race car print A triangles
   and solid black A triangles in six horizontal rows,
   alternating the triangles and beginning and ending
   each row with a B triangle.

2. Refer to Assemble the Quilt Center on *page 11*,
   Step 2, to assemble the pieced quilt center. The

continued

pieced quilt center should measure 48½×42½", including the seam allowances.

Assemble and Add the Borders

1. Sew together the solid yellow, red, green, and blue 2×9" strips end to end with diagonal seams to make the following:
   - 2—2×53" inner border strips
   - 2—2×47" inner border strips

2. With midpoints aligned, sew the short pieced inner border strips to the side edges of the pieced quilt center, beginning and ending the seams ¼" from the corners. Then add the long pieced inner border strips to the top and bottom edges of the pieced quilt center in the same manner.

3. Miter the corners. For information on mitering corners, see the instructions in Quilter's Schoolhouse, which begins on *page 150*. Press all the seam allowances toward the inner border.

4. Sew the black-and-white flag print 6½×45½" outer border strips to the side edges of the pieced quilt center. Then add the black-and-white flag print 6½×63½" outer border strips to the top and bottom edges of the pieced quilt center to complete the quilt top. Press all seam allowances toward the outer border.

Complete the Quilt

1. Layer the quilt top, batting, and backing according to the instructions in Quilter's Schoolhouse. Quilt as desired.

2. Use the solid black 2½×42" strips to bind the quilt according to the instructions in Quilter's Schoolhouse.

Triangles in a Triangle

RACE CAR PILLOW

Primary colors wave amid black-and-white checks on this colorful pillow. The race car print on the back carries out the theme.

Materials

⅓ yard *each* of solid red, yellow, green, and blue

½ yard of black-and-white flag print

½ yard of solid black for sashing and border

2 yards of red race car print for backing

41×42" of muslin for lining

41×42" of quilt batting

36" square pillow form

Finished pillow cover: 35×35½"

Cut the Fabrics

To make the best use of your fabrics, cut the pieces in the order that follows. This project uses "Triangles in a Triangle" Pattern B on *Pattern Sheet 1.* To make a template of the pattern, follow the instructions in Quilter's Schoolhouse, which begins on *page 150.*

From *each* solid red, yellow, green, and blue, cut:
• 8 of Pattern B reversed

From black-and-white flag print, cut:
• 32 of Pattern B reversed

From solid black, cut:
• 2—2×36" border strips
• 5—2×32½" sashing and border strips

From red race car print, cut:
• 2—36×42" rectangles

Assemble the Pillow Center

1. Lay out four horizontal rows of eight solid color B reversed triangles and eight black-and-white flag print B reversed triangles.

2. Sew together the triangles in each row. Press the seam allowances in one direction. Lay out the four pieced rows and three solid black 2×32½" sashing strips; sew together to make the pillow cover center. Press the seam allowances toward the sashing.

Add the Border

Sew the remaining solid black 2×32½" strips to the top and bottom edges of the pillow cover center. Add the solid black 2×36" border strips to the side edges to complete the pillow cover top. Press the seam allowances toward the border.

Complete the Pillow Cover

1. Layer the pillow cover top, batting, and muslin lining according to the instructions in Quilter's Schoolhouse. Quilt as desired.

2. With wrong sides inside, fold each red race car print 36×42" rectangle in half to form two double-thick 21×36" pieces. Overlap the folded edges by 5". Stitch ¼" from the top and bottom edges, including across the folds, to secure the pieces, and create the pillow cover back.

3. With right sides together, layer the pillow cover top and the pillow cover back. Sew together the pieces along all four edges; turn right side out. Insert the pillow form through the back opening.

The brilliant contrast of regal red and natural muslin gives this traditional pattern a stately look. In the antique quilt shown opposite, exquisite hand quilting adds dimension.

KING SOLOMON'S
Temple

Materials

3¾ yards of muslin for blocks and border

4⅛ yards of solid red for blocks, border, and binding

4½ yards of backing fabric

80" square of quilt batting

Finished quilt top: 74" square
Finished block: 15" square

Quantities specified for 44/45"-wide, 100% cotton fabrics. All measurements include a ¼" seam allowance. Sew with right sides together unless otherwise stated.

Cut the Fabrics

To make the best use of your fabrics, cut the pieces in the order that follows. Letter designations are used in cutting and assembly; there are no pattern pieces for this project.

Cut the border strips the length of the fabric (parallel to the selvage). The border strip measurements are mathematically correct. You may wish to cut your border strips longer than specified to allow for possible sewing differences.

From muslin, cut:
- 2—4½×74½" outer border strips
- 2—4½×66½" outer border strips
- 288—2⅜" squares, cutting each in half diagonally for a total of 576 triangles for position A
- 32—6³⁄₁₆" squares, cutting each in half diagonally for a total of 64 triangles for position D
- 96—2" squares for position B

From solid red, cut:
- 4—2×76" binding strips
- 2—3½×66½" inner border strips
- 2—3½×60½" inner border strips
- 352—2⅜" squares, cutting each in half diagonally for a total of 704 triangles for position A
- 32—5⅜" squares, cutting each in half diagonally for a total of 64 triangles for position E
- 16—5" squares for position C
- 32—2" squares for position B

continued

Assemble the King Solomon's Temple Blocks

1. Join one muslin A triangle and one solid red A triangle to make a triangle-square (see Diagram 1). Press the seam allowance toward the red triangle. The triangle-square should measure 2" square, including the seam allowances. Repeat to make a total of 576 triangle-squares.

Diagram 1

2. Referring to Diagram 2 for placement, lay out 36 triangle-squares, one solid red C square, six muslin B squares, two solid red B squares, four muslin D triangles, eight solid red A triangles, and four solid red E triangles.

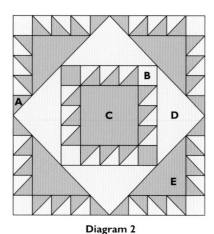

Diagram 2

3. Starting in the center of the layout, sew together two vertical rows of three triangle-squares each (see Diagram 3). Press the seam allowances in one direction. Then join the pieced rows to opposite edges of the solid red C square. Press seam allowances toward the solid red C square.

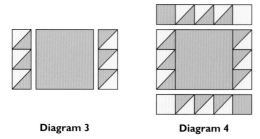

Diagram 3   **Diagram 4**

4. Referring to Diagram 4, sew together two horizontal rows of three triangle-squares each. Press the seam allowances in one direction.

Then join a muslin B square and a solid red B square to opposite ends of the pieced rows. Press the seam allowances toward the squares. Join the rows to the remaining raw edges of the solid red C square to make the center unit. Press the seam allowances toward the solid red C square.

5. Sew the long edges of two muslin D triangles to opposite edges of the center unit (see Diagram 5). Press the seam allowances toward the large triangles. Add muslin D triangles to the remaining raw edges of the center unit. Press the seam allowances toward the large triangles. The pieced center unit should now measure 11⅛" square, including the seam allowances.

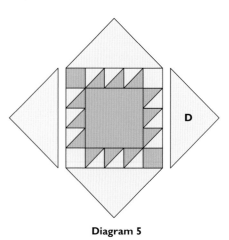

Diagram 5

6. Sew together three triangle-squares and one solid red A triangle in a vertical row as shown in Diagram 6. Press the seam allowances in one direction. Add the pieced row to a solid red E triangle. Press the seam allowance toward the solid red E triangle.

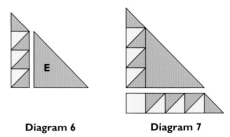

Diagram 6   **Diagram 7**

7. Referring to Diagram 7, sew together three triangle-squares, one solid red A triangle, and one muslin B square in a horizontal row. Press the seam allowances toward the muslin square. Add the pieced row to the solid red E triangle to make a corner unit. Press the seam allowance toward the solid red E triangle. Repeat to make a total of four corner units.

8. Sew the long edges of two corner units to opposite edges of the center unit (see Diagram 8). Press the seam allowances toward the center unit. Add corner units to the remaining raw edges of the center unit to make a block. Press the seam allowances toward the center unit to complete a King Solomon's Temple block. The pieced block should measure 15½" square, including the seam allowances.

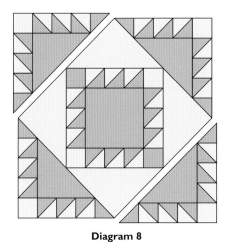

Diagram 8

9. Repeat steps 2 through 8 to make a total of 16 King Solomon's Temple blocks.

Assemble the Quilt Center

1. Referring to the photograph *above right*, lay out the 16 blocks in four rows. Sew together the blocks in each row. Press the seam allowances in one direction, alternating the direction with each row.

2. Join the rows to complete the quilt center. Press the seam allowances in one direction. The pieced quilt center should measure 60½" square, including the seam allowances.

Add the Borders

1. Sew a solid red 3½×60½" inner border strip to opposite edges of the quilt center. Then add a solid red 3½×66½" inner border strip to the remaining raw edges of the quilt center. Press the seam allowances toward the inner border strips.

2. Sew a muslin 4½×66½" outer border strip to opposite edges of the quilt center. Then add a muslin 4½×74½" outer border strip to the remaining raw edges of the quilt center to complete the quilt top. Press the seam allowances toward the outer border strips.

Complete the Quilt

1. Layer the quilt top, batting, and backing according to the instructions in Quilter's Schoolhouse, which begins on *page 150*.

2. Quilt as desired. The quilt shown was outline-quilted around each A triangle and B square and diagonally through the B squares. Then diagonal crosshatching was added, with parallel lines ½" apart, in the C squares and D and E triangles.

To quilt the borders, draw parallel lines 1" apart at a 45° angle from the edge. Then add a parallel line halfway between every previously drawn line. Quilt on the drawn lines.

3. Use the solid red 2×76" binding strips to bind the quilt according to the instructions in Quilter's Schoolhouse.

continued

King Solomon's Temple
optional sizes

If you'd like to make this quilt in a size other than for a throw, use the information *below.*

Alternate quilt sizes	Twin	Full/Queen	King
Number of blocks	15	30	36
Number of blocks wide by long	3×5	5×6	6×6
Finished size	59×89"	89×104"	104" square
Yardage requirements			
Muslin	3¾ yards	6½ yards	7½ yards
Solid red	4½ yards	7¼ yards	8¼ yards
Backing	5¼ yards	8 yards	7½ yards
Batting	65×95"	95×110"	110" square

TWIN QUILT

Create a sunny aura with cheerful prints. The controlled placement of triangle-squares in a rainbow of colors results in the same geometric pattern as the two-color quilt.

Materials

2¾ yards of white print for blocks

3⅛ yards total of assorted pink, red, yellow, peach, green, blue, and lavender prints for blocks

2¼ yards of yellow print for border

⅝ yard of blue print for binding

5⅓ yards of backing fabric

66×96" of quilt batting

Finished quilt top: 60×90"

Cut the Fabrics

To make the best use of your fabrics, cut the pieces in the order that follows. The border strips are cut the length of the fabric (parallel to the selvage).

The assorted prints have been placed to create secondary blocks on the quilt top (see the photograph *opposite* and the Quilt Assembly Diagram on *page 24*). Four different prints were used in each block. When you lay out the quilt center, bring together the block corners in the same prints to form a secondary block design.

From white print, cut:
- 30—6³⁄₁₆" squares, cutting each in half diagonally for a total of 60 triangles for position D
- 294—2³⁄₈" squares, cutting each in half diagonally for a total of 588 triangles for position A
- 98—2" squares for position B

From assorted prints, cut:
- 30—5³⁄₈" squares, cutting each in half diagonally for a total of 60 triangles for position E
- 19—5" squares for position C
- 354—2³⁄₈" squares, cutting each in half diagonally for a total of 708 triangles for position A
- 38—2" squares for position B

From yellow print, cut:
- 2—8×75½" border strips
- 2—8×45½" border strips

From blue print, cut:
- 8—2½×42" binding strips

Assemble the King Solomon's Temple Blocks

1. Referring to the Assemble the King Solomon's Temple Blocks instructions on *page 20* and the Quilt Assembly Diagram on *page 24*, use the white print A triangles and the assorted print A triangles to make a total of 588 triangle-squares.

2. Referring to the same assembly instructions, use 36 triangle-squares, one assorted print C square, six white print B squares, two assorted print B squares, four white print D triangles, eight assorted print A triangles, and four E triangles in different prints to make a King Solomon's Temple block. The A triangles and triangle-squares should match their adjacent E triangles (see the Quilt Assembly Diagram). Repeat to make a total of 15 King Solomon's Temple blocks, considering carefully the placement of the E triangles so your layout will result in a secondary block

design. Arranging the blocks on a design wall as you complete each one will help you determine color placement.

3. Referring to the same assembly instructions, use 12 triangle-squares, one assorted print C square, two white print B squares, and two assorted print B squares to make a pieced corner block (see Diagram 4 on *page 20*). The pieced corner block should measure 8" square, including the seam allowances. Repeat to make a total of four pieced corner blocks.

Assemble the Quilt Center

1. Referring to the Quilt Assembly Diagram for placement, lay out the 15 King Solomon's Temple blocks in five rows. Sew together the blocks in each row. Press the seam allowances in one direction, alternating the direction with each row.

continued

2. Join the rows to complete the quilt center. Press the seam allowances in one direction. The pieced quilt center should measure 45½×75½", including the seam allowances.

Add the Border

Sew a yellow print 8×45½" border strip to the top and bottom edges of the pieced quilt center. Join a pieced corner block to each end of the yellow print 8×75½" border strips. Sew one pieced border strip to each side edge of the pieced quilt center to complete the quilt top. Press the seam allowances toward the border.

Complete the Quilt

1. Layer the quilt top, batting, and backing according to the instructions in Quilter's Schoolhouse, which begins on *page 150*. Quilt as desired.

Quilt Assembly Diagram

2. Use the blue print 2½×42" strips to bind the quilt according to the instructions in Quilter's Schoolhouse.

PILLOW SHAM

Use scraps from the quilt to create this delightful pillow sham. Spare squares compose the center; triangle-squares frame it.

Materials

¼ yard of white print for sham front

¾ yard total of assorted prints for sham front

1¾ yards of blue print for sham back and flange

¾ yard of muslin for lining

27×36" of quilt batting

20×29" pillow

Finished pillow sham: 34×25"

Cut the Fabrics

To make the best use of your fabrics, cut the pieces in the order that follows.

From white print, cut:
- 30—2⅜" squares, cutting each in half diagonally for a total of 60 triangles
- 2—2" squares

From assorted prints, cut:
- 24—5" squares
- 30—2⅜" squares, cutting each in half diagonally for a total of 60 triangles
- 2—2" squares

From blue print, cut:
- 2—25½×40" rectangles
- 2—2½×34½" strips
- 2—2½×21½" strips

Assemble the Pillow Sham

1. Referring to Assemble the King Solomon's Temple Blocks on *page 20,* use the white print triangles and the assorted print triangles to make a total of 60 triangle-squares.

2. Referring to the photograph *above,* lay out 24 assorted print 5" squares in four horizontal rows. Sew together the squares in each row. Press the seam allowances in one direction, alternating the direction with each row. Then join the rows to make the center unit.

3. Sew together 18 triangle-squares to make a top border unit. Press the seam allowances in one direction. Repeat to make a bottom border unit. Join the border units to the top and bottom edges of the center unit with the white triangles pointing toward the center.

4. Sew together 12 triangle-squares, adding an assorted print B square at one end and a white print B square to the other to make a side border unit. Repeat to make a second side border unit. Join the units to the side edges of the center unit to complete the pillow sham front. Press the seam allowances in one direction. The pieced pillow sham front should measure 30½×21½", including the seam allowances.

5. Layer the pillow sham front, batting, and muslin according to the instructions in Quilter's Schoolhouse, which begins on *page 150.* Quilt as desired.

6. Sew a blue print 2½×21½" strip to each side edge of the quilted pillow sham front. Then join a blue print 2½×34½" strip to the top and bottom edges of the quilted pillow sham front to complete the pillow sham top. Press all seam allowances toward the blue strips. The pillow sham top should measure 34½×25½", including the seam allowances.

7. With wrong sides inside, fold each blue print 25½×40" rectangle in half to form two double-thick 20×25½" pieces. Overlap the folded edges by 5". Stitch ¼" from the top and bottom edges, including across the folds, to secure the pieces and create the pillow sham back.

8. With right sides together, layer the pillow sham top and the back. Sew the pieces together along all four edges to complete the pillow sham; turn right side out. Press the sham, making sure the corner points are sharp. Stitch in the ditch just inside the blue print flange. Insert the pillow through the back opening.

FRAMED QUILTS

Safari prints lend an ethnic look

to framed blocks.

Materials for Option I

¼ yard of orange tiger print for block

⅜ yard of black print for block and binding

¼ yard of yellow leopard print for block

¼ yard of black-and-white print for block and
    inner border

½ yard of animal print for block and outer border

29" square of backing fabric

29" square of quilt batting

Mat and frame

Finished quilt top: 23" square

Cut the Fabrics

To make the best use of your fabrics, cut the pieces
in the order that follows.

From orange tiger print, cut:
- 22—2⅜" squares, cutting each in half diagonally
  for a total of 44 triangles for position A
- 2—2" squares for position B

From black print, cut:
- 18—2⅜" squares, cutting each in half diagonally
  for a total of 36 triangles for position A
- 3—2½×42" binding strips
- 6—2" squares for position B

From yellow leopard print, cut:
- 2—6³⁄₁₆" squares, cutting each in half diagonally
  for a total of 4 triangles for position D

From black-and-white print, cut:
- 2—5⅜" squares, cutting each in half diagonally
  for a total of 4 triangles for position E
- 2—1×16½" inner border strips
- 2—1×15½" inner border strips

From animal print, cut:
- 1—5" square for position C
- 2—4×23½" outer border strips
- 2—4×16½" outer border strips

Assemble the King Solomon's Temple Block

1. Referring to the Assemble the King Solomon's
   Temple Blocks instructions on *page 20*, use the
   orange tiger print A triangles and the black print
   A triangles to make a total of 36 triangle-squares.

2. Referring to the same assembly instructions
   and the top framed piece in the photograph
   above left, use the 36 triangle-squares, one
   animal print C square, six black print B squares,
   two orange tiger print B squares, four yellow
   leopard print D triangles, eight orange tiger print
   A triangles, and four black-and-white print
   E triangles to make one King Solomon's
   Temple block.

Add the Borders

1. Sew a black-and-white print 1×15½" inner border
   strip to each side edge of the pieced block. Then
   join a black-and-white print 1×16½" inner border
   strip to the top and bottom edges of the pieced

block. Press the seam allowances toward the inner border.

2. Sew an animal print 4×16½" outer border strip to each side edge of the pieced block. Then join an animal print 4×23½" outer border strip to the top and bottom edges of the pieced block to complete the quilt top. Press the seam allowances toward the outer border.

Complete the Quilt

1. Layer the quilt top, batting, and backing as instructed in Quilter's Schoolhouse, which begins on *page 150*. Quilt as desired.

2. Use the black print 2½×42" strips to bind the quilt according to the instructions in Quilter's Schoolhouse. Mat and frame as desired.

Materials for Option II

⅜ yard of black print for block and binding

¼ yard of yellow leopard print for block

¼ yard of orange tiger print for block

¼ yard of black-and-white print for block and inner border

½ yard of animal print for block and outer border

29" square of backing fabric

29" square of quilt batting

Mat and frame

Finished quilt top: 23" square

Cut the Fabrics

To make the best use of your fabrics, cut the pieces in the order that follows.

From black print, cut:

• 22—2⅜" squares, cutting each in half diagonally for a total of 44 triangles for position A
• 3—2½×42" binding strips
• 2—2" squares for position B

From yellow leopard print, cut:

• 18—2⅜" squares, cutting each in half diagonally for a total of 36 triangles for position A
• 6—2" squares for position B

From orange tiger print, cut:

• 2—5⅜" squares, cutting each in half diagonally for a total of 4 triangles for position E

From black-and-white print, cut:

• 2—6³⁄₁₆" squares, cutting each in half diagonally for a total of 4 triangles for position D
• 2—1×16½" inner border strips
• 2—1×15½" inner border strips

From animal print, cut:

• 1—5" square for position C
• 2—4×23½" outer border strips
• 2—4×16½" outer border strips

Assemble the King Solomon's Temple Block

1. Referring to the Assemble the King Solomon's Temple Blocks instructions on *page 20*, use the black print A triangles and the yellow leopard print A triangles to make a total of 36 triangle-squares.

2. Referring to the same assembly instructions and the bottom framed piece in the photograph *opposite,* use the 36 triangle-squares, one animal print C square, six yellow leopard print B squares, two black print B squares, four black-and-white print D triangles, eight black print A triangles, and four orange tiger print E triangles to make one King Solomon's Temple block.

Add the Borders

Referring to the Add the Borders instructions *opposite*, add the inner and outer border strips to the pieced block to make the quilt top.

Complete the Quilt

1. Layer the quilt top, batting, and backing as instructed in Quilter's Schoolhouse, which begins on *page 150*. Quilt as desired.

2. Use the black print 2½×42" strips to bind the quilt according to the instructions in Quilter's Schoolhouse. Mat and frame as desired.

This antique quilt glows with the faint pink of a new rose. Indeed,

it is the pink chambray that dates the quilt to the 1920s. Re-create it in any

two colors for an heirloom quilt with timeless appeal.

Checkerboard

Materials

4¾ yards of off-white print for blocks

4 yards of solid pink for blocks, border, and binding

5½ yards of backing fabric

82×97" of quilt batting

Quantities specified for 44/45"-wide, 100% cotton fabrics. All measurements include a ¼" seam allowance. Sew with right sides together unless otherwise stated.

Finished quilt top: 76½×81½"
Finished block: 13½" square

continued

Select the Fabrics

In this antique quilt, Checkerboard blocks alternate with setting blocks. The pink is chambray, a fabric woven with colored threads running one way and white threads running the other way. The off-white cotton is printed with tiny black dots.

To replicate the vintage look of this quilt, use a shirting print for the off-white fabric.

Cut the Fabrics

To make the best use of your fabrics, cut the pieces in the order that follows.

From off-white print, cut:
- 46—2×42" strips
- 9—6" squares
- 48—4½" squares
- 2—10⅜" squares, cutting each in half diagonally for a total of 4 corner triangles
- 3—9" squares, cutting each diagonally twice in an X for a total of 12 large triangles
- 6—6⅞" squares, cutting each diagonally twice in an X for a total of 24 small triangles

From solid pink, cut:
- 2—5½×42" strips
- 44—2×42" strips for strip sets and binding
- 20—1¾×42" strips

Assemble the Checkerboard Blocks

1. Aligning long edges and referring to diagrams 1 and 2, join the off-white print and solid pink 2×42" strips to make four of Strip Set A and four of Strip Set B. Press the seam allowances toward the pink strips.

2. Cut each strip set into 2"-wide segments. You'll need a total of 80 Strip Set A segments and 64 Strip Set B segments.

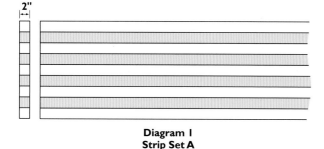

Diagram 1
Strip Set A

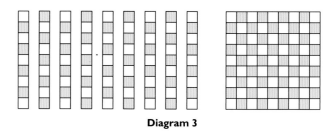

Diagram 2
Strip Set B

3. Referring to Diagram 3, lay out five Strip Set A segments and four Strip Set B segments. Join the segments to make a Checkerboard block as shown. Press the seam allowances in one direction. The pieced Checkerboard block should measure 14" square, including the seam allowances. Repeat to make a total of 16 blocks.

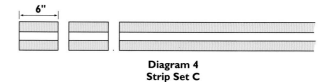

Diagram 3

Assemble the Setting Blocks and Triangles

1. Referring to Diagram 4, join two solid pink 1¾"-wide strips and one off-white print 2"-wide strip to make a Strip Set C. Press the seam allowances toward the pink strips. Repeat to make a total of 10 strip sets.

Diagram 4
Strip Set C

2. Cut each strip set into 6"-wide segments. You'll need a total of 68 Strip Set C segments.

3. Referring to Diagram 5, lay out one off-white print 6" square, four off-white print 4½" squares, and four Strip Set C segments in rows. Join the units in each row. Press the seam allowances away from the Strip Set C segments. Join the rows to make a pieced setting block. Press the seam

allowances away from the center. The pieced setting block should measure 14" square, including the seam allowances. Repeat to make a total of nine pieced setting blocks.

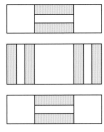

Diagram 5

4. Referring to Diagram 6, lay out one off-white print 4½" square, one off-white print large triangle, two off-white print small triangles, and two Strip Set C segments. Join the units in each row. Press the seam allowances away from the Strip Set C segments. Join the rows to make a pieced setting triangle. Press the seam allowances in one direction. Repeat to make a total of 12 pieced setting triangles.

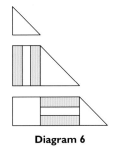

Diagram 6

Assemble the Quilt Top

1. Lay out the 16 Checkerboard blocks, the nine setting blocks, the 12 setting triangles, and the four off-white print corner triangles in diagonal rows as shown in the Quilt Assembly Diagram (the heavy black lines on the diagram indicate the rows).

2. Sew together the pieces in each row, except for the corner triangles. Press the seam allowances toward the setting units. Join the rows, adding the corner triangles last, to complete the quilt center. Press the seam allowances in one direction. The pieced quilt center should measure 77" square, including the seam allowances.

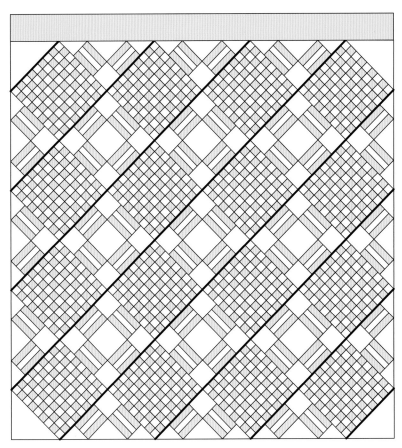

Quilt Assembly Diagram

Add the Border

1. Cut and piece two solid pink 5½×42" strips to make a 5½×77" border strip.

2. Sew the border strip to the top edge of the quilt center to complete the quilt top. Press the seam allowance toward the border strip.

Complete the Quilt

1. Layer the quilt top, batting, and backing according to the instructions in Quilter's Schoolhouse, which begins on *page 150.*

2. Quilt as desired. The quilt shown was quilted in an allover fan pattern.

3. Use the remaining solid pink 2×42" strips to bind the quilt according to the instructions in Quilter's Schoolhouse.

continued

Checkerboard Quilt
optional sizes

If you'd like to make this quilt in a size other than for a double bed, use the information *below*. The measurements and yardage requirements for the wall and king-size quilts do not include the single top border found in the original quilt.

Alternate quilt sizes	Wall	Twin	King
Number of blocks	4	12	36
Number of blocks wide by long	2×2	3×4	6×6
Finished size	57⅜" square (no border)	57×81" (one border)	114¾" square (no border)
Yardage requirements			
Off-white print	1⅝ yards	3⅝ yards	8⅞ yards
Solid pink	1¼ yards	3⅜ yards	7½ yards
Backing	1¼ yards	4⅞ yards	10 yards
Batting	45" square	64×87"	120" square

optional colors

In this wall hanging, one light blue print and assorted dark blue prints compose the Checkerboard blocks. The brown print and white floral of the setting squares complete the vintage color palette. The blocks are set square with the borders, which eliminates the need for corner triangles and partial setting blocks.

TOTE BAG

Perfect for quilting supplies as well as treks to the grocery or library, this

Checkerboard tote is as practical to use as it is easy to make. Select two favorite

fabrics for the bottom portion, two for the middle band, and three for the strips

at the top. Include bold bands of a contrasting color for a multihued palette.

Materials

⅝ yard of beige print No.1 for bottom

    checkerboard section

⅝ yard of blue plaid for bottom

    checkerboard section

⅛ yard of beige print No. 2 for middle

    checkerboard section

⅛ yard of blue print for middle checkerboard section

¼ yard of brown print for bands and handles

⅛ yard of tan plaid for top section

⅛ yard of beige print No. 3 for top section

⅛ yard of blue stripe for top section

1¼ yards of coordinating print for lining and pockets

2×42" of interfacing for handle

24×50" of muslin for backing

24×50" of quilt batting

Finished tote: 18×20¼"

continued

Cut the Fabrics

To make the best use of your fabrics, cut the pieces in the order that follows.

From beige print No. 1, cut:
- 8—2×42" strips

From blue plaid, cut:
- 8—2×42" strips

From beige print No. 2, cut:
- 2—2×42" strips

From blue print, cut:
- 2—2×42" strips

From brown print, cut:
- 4—1¼×18½" strips
- 1—4×42" strip

From tan plaid, cut:
- 2—1¾×42" strips

From beige print No. 3, cut:
- 2—1¾×42" strips

From blue stripe, cut:
- 2—1¾×42" strips

From coordinating print, cut:
- 2—18½×22½" rectangles
- 2—13×17" rectangles

Make the Tote Bag Sections

1. Referring to the Assemble the Checkerboard Blocks instructions on *page 30*, Step 1, use the beige print No. 1 and blue plaid 2×42" strips to make two of Strip Set A (see Diagram 1 on *page 30*). *Note:* The tote bag strip sets each have eight strips rather than nine.

2. Cut each strip set into 2"-wide segments. You'll need a total of 24 Strip Set A segments.

3. Referring to Diagram 1, lay out 12 Strip Set A segments, alternating the color placement. Join the segments to make a bottom checkerboard section. The bottom checkerboard section should measure 12×18½", including the seam allowances. Repeat to make a second bottom checkerboard section.

4. Use the beige print No. 2 and the blue print 2×42" strips to make a total of two strip sets. Cut the strip sets into 2"-wide segments. You'll need a total of 24 segments. Join 12 segments in a row, alternating the color placement, to make a middle checkerboard section (see Diagram 1). The middle checkerboard section should measure

5×18½", including the seam allowances. Repeat to make a second middle checkerboard section. Sew a brown print 1¼×18½" strip to each long edge of the middle checkerboard sections.

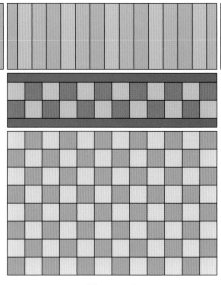

Diagram 1

5. To make the top sections, refer to Assemble the Setting Blocks and Triangles on *page 30*, Step 1. Use one tan plaid, one beige print No. 3, and one blue stripe 1¾×42" strip to make a Strip Set C. Make a total of two strip sets.

6. Cut the strip sets into a total of ten 6"-wide segments as shown in Diagram 4 on *page 30*. Join five Strip Set C segments to make a top section. The top section should measure 6×19¼", including the seam allowances. Repeat to make a second top section.

Assemble the Tote

1. Referring to Diagram 1, join a bottom and middle checkerboard section. Center a top section on the middle checkerboard section; sew together and trim to fit to make a tote panel. The tote panel should measure 18½×48", including the seam allowances. Repeat to make a second tote panel. Sew the tote panels together along the bottom edges.

2. Layer the joined tote panels, batting, and muslin backing as instructed in Quilter's Schoolhouse, which begins on *page 150*. Quilt as desired. Fold the joined tote panels at the bottom seam with

the right side inside; make a 3" inverted pleat at the bottom of each side (see Diagram 2). Sew the side seams. Turn right side out; the tote should have a flat bottom (see Diagram 3).

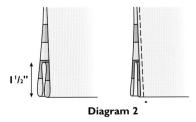

Diagram 2

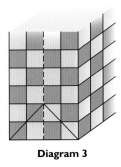

Diagram 3

3. Turn under a short edge of a coordinating print 13×17" rectangle ¼"; press. Fold down 1" and top-stitch to hem a pocket. Fold under the three remaining edges ¼"; press. Place the prepared pocket atop the right side of a coordinating print 18½×22½" rectangle 2" from the top edge (see Diagram 4). Stitch the pocket in place. Repeat to add a pocket to the remaining coordinating print 18½×22½" rectangle.

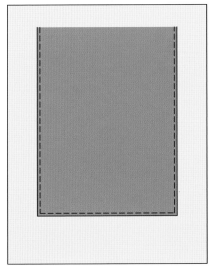

Diagram 4

4. With right sides together, sew the coordinating print 18½×22½" rectangles, making a 3" inverted pleat in the bottom of each side seam to make the lining. Leave a 5" opening in one side seam.

5. Slip the prepared lining into the quilted tote, aligning top edges and side seams; pin.

6. Fold the long edges of the brown print 4×42" strip so they meet at the center with the wrong side inside (see Diagram 5); press. Place the interfacing 2"-wide strip inside the folded strip. Then fold the strip in half lengthwise, encasing the interfacing; press. Topstitch along the strip's long edges. Cut the strip into two 21"-long handles.

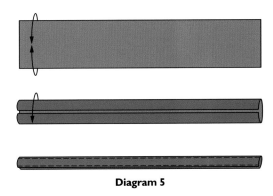

Diagram 5

7. Slip the handles between the quilted tote and lining (see Diagram 6). Align raw edges and position the handle ends 4½" from the side seams; pin in place. Stitch around the top edge with a ½" seam allowance. Turn right side out through the opening in the side seam; hand-stitch the opening closed. Push the lining back into the bag. Topstitch along the upper edge of the tote.

Diagram 6

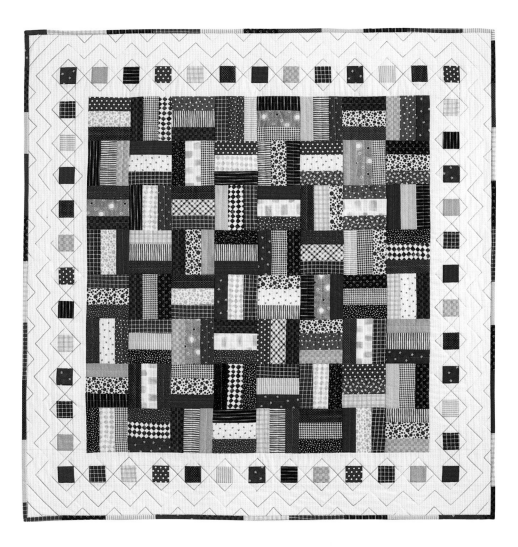

BABY QUILT

Assorted prints in pure primary colors set up

a checkerboard of an entirely different

nature in this quilt for a little one.

Materials

1⅓ yards of solid white for borders

2 yards total of assorted red, yellow, and blue prints

    for blocks, pieced border, and binding

2¾ yards of backing fabric

50" square of quilt batting

Finished quilt top: 43½" square

Cut the Fabrics

To make the best use of your fabrics, cut the pieces in the order that follows. The borders are cut lengthwise (parallel to the selvage).

From solid white, cut:
- 2—3½×44" outer border strips
- 2—3½×38" outer border strips
- 2—1¾×35" inner border strips
- 2—1¾×32½" inner border strips
- 48—2" squares

From assorted prints, cut:
- 8—2×42" strips
- 16—1¾×42" strips
- 48—2" squares

Assemble the Segments

1. Referring to the Assemble the Setting Blocks and Triangles instructions on *page 30*, Step 1, Diagram 4, use two assorted print 1¾×42" strips and one assorted print 2×42" strip to make a Strip Set C. Repeat to make a total of eight strip sets.

2. Cut each strip set into 4½"-wide segments. You'll need a total of 64 Strip Set C segments.

Assemble the Quilt Center

1. Referring to the photograph *opposite* for placement, lay out the 64 segments in eight rows. Sew together the segments in each row. Press the seam allowances in one direction, alternating the direction with each row.

2. Join the rows to make the quilt center. Press the seam allowances in one direction. The pieced quilt center should measure 32½" square, including the seam allowances.

Assemble and Add the Borders

1. Sew the solid white 1¾×32½" inner border strips to opposite edges of the pieced quilt center. Then join the solid white 1¾×35" inner border strips to the remaining edges of the pieced quilt center. Press all seam allowances toward the border.

2. Join 12 of the solid white 2" squares and 11 of the assorted print 2" squares, alternating color placement, to make a 2×35" short pieced border strip. Repeat to make a second short pieced border strip. Sew the short pieced border strips to opposite edges of the pieced quilt center. Press the seam allowances toward the pieced border.

3. Sew together 12 of the solid white 2" squares and 13 of the assorted print 2" squares, alternating color placement, to make a 2×38" long pieced border strip. Repeat to make a second strip. Join the long pieced border strips to the remaining edges of the pieced quilt center. Press the seam allowances toward the pieced border.

4. Sew the solid white 3½×38" outer border strips to opposite edges of the pieced quilt center. Then join the solid white 3½×44" outer border strips to the remaining edges of the pieced quilt center to complete the quilt top. Press the seam allowances toward the pieced border.

Complete the Quilt

From assorted prints, cut:

- Enough 2½"-wide pieces in lengths varying from 4½" to 6½" to total 180" in length

1. Layer the quilt top, batting, and backing according to the instructions in Quilter's Schoolhouse, which begins on *page 150*. Quilt as desired.

2. Piece the assorted print 2½"-wide pieces into a strip 180" long. Use the pieced strip to bind the quilt according to the instructions in Quilter's Schoolhouse.

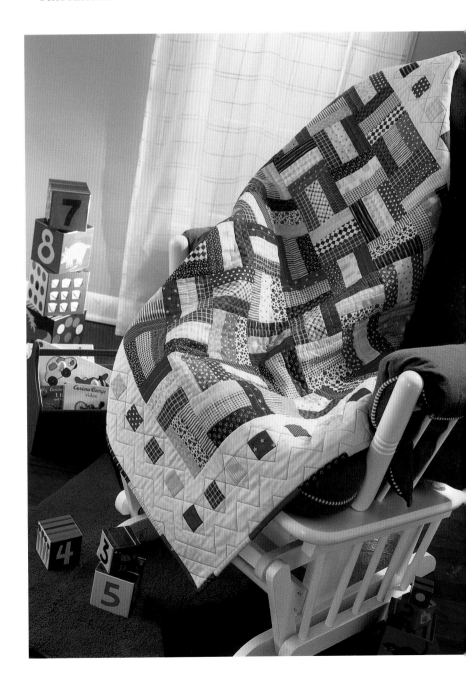

ROUND
ABOUT

The circle and the arcs within the circle have piqued the interest of quiltmakers for ages.

The gentle curves that form "Spring Leaves," the quarter circles that anchor "Railroad Crossing," and the circular patterns that weave through "Apple Core" illustrate the endless options this round shape offers.

The myriad methods—hand- or machine-piecing, fusible web, and foundation piecing—will perfect your curved piecing skills.

SPRING *Leaves*

When Jan Wildman designed this quilt,

she was thinking spring. A leaf shape,

multiple green prints, and the delicate hues

of the season's first blossoms brought her

idea to life.

Spring Leaves

Materials

1¼ yards total of assorted pink prints for blocks

1¼ yards total of assorted yellow prints for blocks

2 yards total of assorted green prints for blocks,
    sashing, and border

1⅛ yards of light yellow print for sashing
    and border

½ yard of lime green print for binding

3 yards of backing fabric

66×55" of quilt batting

Finished quilt top: 59½×48½"
Finished block: 10" square

Quantities specified for 44/45"-wide, 100% cotton
fabrics. All measurements include a ¼" seam
allowance. Sew with right sides together unless
otherwise stated.

Cut the Fabrics

The patterns are on *Pattern Sheet 2*. To make
templates of the patterns, follow the instructions in
Quilter's Schoolhouse, which begins on *page 150*.

    If you want to use a rotary cutter to cut your
fabrics, make sure your pattern templates are made
of thick plastic or cardboard. If you choose to use
scissors for cutting, be sure to trace the template first
onto fabric. Mark the center matching points on the
A and B pieces as shown on the patterns.

continued

From assorted pink prints, cut:
- 40—6" squares, cutting each in half diagonally for a total of 80 triangles

From assorted yellow prints, cut:
- 40—6" squares, cutting each in half diagonally for a total of 80 triangles

From assorted green prints, cut:
- 80—4¾" squares, cutting each in half diagonally for a total of 160 triangles
- 4—3¼" squares for border
- 14—1½×3¼" rectangles for border
- 12—1½" squares for sashing

From light yellow print, cut:
- 18—3¼×10½" strips for border
- 31—1½×10½" strips for sashing

From lime green print, cut:
- 6—2½×42" binding strips

Assemble the Blocks

1. Place Pattern A atop a pink print triangle; cut along the curved edge to make a background piece (see Diagram 1). Repeat with the remaining pink print triangles and all the yellow print triangles.

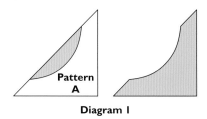

Diagram 1

2. Place Pattern B atop a green print triangle; cut along the curved edge to make a leaf piece (see Diagram 2). Repeat with the remaining green print triangles.

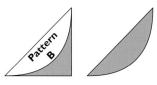

Diagram 2

3. Layer a pink print background piece and a green print leaf piece; match the center marks on the curved edges (see Diagram 3). Using slender pins and picking up only a few threads at a time, pin at the center, then each end; pin generously in between (see Diagram 4).

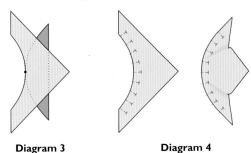

Diagram 3 **Diagram 4**

Sew together the pieces, removing each pin just before your needle reaches it, to make a leaf subunit (see Diagram 5). Press the seam allowance toward the green print leaf piece. Repeat to make a total of 160 leaf subunits (80 with pink print background pieces and 80 with yellow print background pieces).

Diagram 5

4. Sew together one pink print leaf subunit and one yellow print leaf subunit to make a leaf unit (see Diagram 6). Press the seam allowance in one direction. Trim the leaf unit to measure 5½" square, including the seam allowances. Repeat to make a total of 80 leaf units.

Diagram 6

5. Referring to Diagram 7, lay out four leaf units in two rows; sew together the units in pairs. Press the seam allowances in opposite directions. Then join the pairs to make a leaf block. Press the seam allowance in one direction. The pieced leaf block should measure 10½" square, including the seam allowances. Repeat to make a total of 20 leaf blocks.

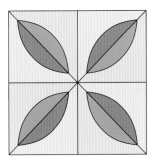

Diagram 7

Assemble the Quilt Top

1. Referring to the photograph *opposite* for placement, lay out the 20 pieced blocks and the green print and light yellow print sashing and border pieces in nine horizontal rows.

2. Sew together the pieces in each row. Press the seam allowances toward the light yellow print strips. Then join the rows to complete the quilt top. Press the seam allowances in one direction.

Complete the Quilt

1. Layer the quilt top, batting, and backing according to the instructions in Quilter's Schoolhouse, which begins on *page 150*.

2. Quilt as desired. See Machine-Quilting Tips on *page 44*. Designer Jan Wildman machine-quilted an allover pattern of free-form leaves on vines. Jan started the vines along the bottom edge of the quilt and quilted toward the top edge. Tendrils extend from the main vines in all directions.

To stitch Jan's leaves and vine pattern, refer to the photograph *below*. Begin by stitching a portion of the vine. Then curve out to make the top leaf edge and come to a point. Curve back to the vine for the bottom edge of the leaf. Continue in this manner until you've completed a vine.

3. Use the lime green print 2½×42" strips to bind the quilt according to the instructions in Quilter's Schoolhouse.

continued

Spring Leaves Quilt
optional sizes

If you'd like to make this quilt in a size other than for a throw, use the information *below*.

Alternate quilt sizes	Twin	Full/Queen	King
Number of blocks	35	56	81
Number of blocks wide by long	5×7	7×8	9×9
Finished size	59½×81½"	81½×92½"	103½" square
Yardage requirements			
Assorted pink prints	2 yards	3 yards	4½ yards
Assorted yellow prints	2 yards	3 yards	4½ yards
Assorted green prints	2⅞ yards	4⅜ yards	6½ yards
Light yellow print	2 yards	2½ yards	3⅛ yards
Binding	⅝ yard	⅔ yard	⅞ yard
Backing	4⅞ yards	5½ yards	9¼ yards
Batting	66×88"	88×99"	110" square

machine-quilting tips

Quiltmaker Jan Wildman encourages quilters to learn free-motion machine quilting so they easily can add exciting and attractive designs to any quilt. With this technique, you move your quilt in all directions in a controlled manner and let your sewing machine do the stitching. You don't need to mark your quilt top, sew on a drawn line, or create identical symmetrical patterns. Instead you "draw" patterns with your sewing machine needle.

Preparation
When machine-quilting, it's best to have your machine on a large, level work surface so your quilt is properly supported.

To set up your machine for free-motion quilting, cover or lower the feed dogs. Use a darning foot so your quilt can move freely. Make sure your quilt is securely basted, whether with thread, safety pins, or basting spray.

In order to control and move the quilt with as little effort as possible, you need to maximize the friction between your hands and the quilt top. To make your grip "stickier," wear secretary's fingers or quilter's gloves.

Jan suggests choosing either a 100% cotton or an 80% cotton/20% polyester batting. "I find that when using a 100% cotton quilt top, cotton backing, and a cotton batting, all the layers 'stick' together," Jan says. "A 100% polyester batting tends to shift and slide while quilting, and for a beginner that may be frustrating."

Designer Tips
Before starting, Jan suggests reviewing the following machine-quilting tips and practicing on a small sample quilt.

- Select a simple quilting design that can be stitched from one edge of the quilt to the opposite in rows. This eliminates starting and stopping repeatedly.

- Although patterns can run vertically, diagonally, or horizontally across a quilt top, always begin at one edge in the middle of the quilt top and work toward the opposite edge. Continue in this fashion to complete half the quilt top. Then turn the quilt top around and quilt the other half.

- Run the sewing machine at a fairly fast, constant speed, but move your hands in a slow, controlled manner; resist the impulse to move your hands quickly. Use as little hand pressure as necessary to move and control the quilt.

JOURNAL

The simple leaf pattern and buttons make this journal worthy of the

thoughts and remembrances it will hold.

Materials

Scraps of two dark blue prints

Scraps of two light blue prints

Scraps of heavyweight fusible web

Six ½"-diameter buttons

Paper-covered journal

Glue

Cut the Fabrics

This project uses "Spring Leaves" patterns, found on *Pattern Sheet 2*. To use fusible web for appliquéing, as was done in this project, complete the following steps.

1. Lay the fusible web, paper side up, over the patterns. Use a pencil to trace each pattern twice on the dashed lines, leaving ½" between tracings. Cut out each fusible-web piece roughly ¼" outside the traced lines.

2. Following the manufacturer's instructions, press the fusible-web pieces onto the backs of the designated fabrics; let cool. Cut out the shapes on the drawn lines. Peel off the paper backings.

From *each* dark blue print, cut:
- 1 of Pattern A

From *each* light blue print, cut:
- 1 of Pattern B

Assemble the Journal Cover

1. Lay the pieces atop the journal cover as shown in the photograph *above*; fuse in place, using a pressing cloth to protect the journal.

2. Glue three buttons above and three buttons below the leaf block.

BATIK QUILT

A design within the design emerges when "Spring Leaves" blocks are alternated

with setting blocks pieced from four squares each.

Materials

6³⁄₈ yards of assorted dark prints in rust, brown,

    purple, and green for blocks and binding

2½ yards of assorted prints in red, pink, orange,

    and light green for blocks and binding

5⅓ yards of backing fabric

76×96" of quilt batting

Finished quilt top: 70×90"

Cut the Fabrics

To make the best use of your fabrics, cut the pieces in the order that follows. This project uses "Spring Leaves" patterns on *Pattern Sheet 2*. To make templates of these patterns, follow the instructions in Quilter's Schoolhouse, which begins on *page 150*.

From assorted dark prints, cut:

- 132—6" squares, cutting each in half diagonally for a total of 264 triangles
- 120—5½" squares

From assorted prints, cut:

- 132—4¾" squares, cutting each in half diagonally for a total of 264 triangles

Assemble the Blocks

1. Referring to the Assemble the Blocks instructions on *page 42*, Step 1, make a total of 264 dark print background pieces.

2. Referring to the Assemble the Blocks instructions, Step 2, make a total of 264 assorted print leaf pieces.

3. Layer and sew together a dark print background piece and an assorted print leaf piece, referring to the Step 3 instructions on *page 43*, to make a leaf subunit. Make a total of 264 leaf subunits. Sew together the leaf subunits to make a total of 132 leaf units (see Diagram 6 on *page 43*).

4. Refer to the Step 5 instructions to make a leaf block (see Diagram 7 on *page 43*). Repeat to make a total of 18 leaf blocks. Set aside the remaining leaf units for the outer border.

5. Lay out four dark print 5½" squares in two rows of two squares each. Sew together the squares in pairs. Press the seam allowances in opposite directions. Then join the pairs to make a Four-Patch block. The pieced Four-Patch block should measure 10½" square, including the seam

allowances. Repeat to make a total of
17 Four-Patch blocks.

Assemble the Quilt Center

1. Referring to the photograph *opposite*, lay out the
18 leaf blocks and 17 Four-Patch blocks in seven
horizontal rows.

2. Sew together the blocks in each row. Press the
seam allowances toward the Four-Patch blocks.
Then join the rows to make the quilt center. Press
the seam allowances in one direction. The pieced
quilt center should measure 50½×70½", including
the seam allowances.

Add the Inner Pieced Border

1. Sew together 10 dark print 5½" squares to
make the top inner border strip. Press the seam
allowances in one direction. The top inner border
strip should measure 5½×50½", including the
seam allowances. Repeat to make the bottom
inner border strip. Join the pieced strips to the top
and bottom edges of the pieced quilt center. Press
the seam allowances toward the inner border.

2. Sew together 16 dark print 5½" squares to
make a side inner border strip. Press the seam
allowances in one direction. The side inner
border strip should measure 5½×80½", including
the seam allowances. Repeat to make a second
side inner border strip. Join the pieced strips to
the side edges of the pieced quilt center. Press
the seam allowances toward the inner border.

Add the Outer Leaf Border

1. Sew together 12 leaf units to make the top outer
border strip. Press the seam allowances in one
direction. The top outer border strip should
measure 5½×60½", including the seam
allowances. Repeat to make the bottom outer
border strip. Join the pieced strips to the top and
bottom edges of the pieced quilt center. Press
the seam allowances toward the outer border.

2. Sew together 18 leaf units to make a side outer
border strip. Press the seam allowances in one
direction. The side outer border strip should
measure 5½×90½", including the seam
allowances. Repeat to make a second side outer
border strip. Join the pieced strips to the side
edges of the pieced quilt center to complete

the quilt top. Press the seam allowances toward
the outer border.

Complete the Quilt

1. From remaining assorted prints, cut and piece
enough 2½×20" pieces to make a 340"-long
binding strip.

2. Layer the quilt top, batting, and backing according
to the instructions in Quilter's Schoolhouse, which
begins on *page 150*. Quilt as desired.

3. Use the assorted print 2½"-wide pieced strip to
bind the quilt according to the instructions in
Quilter's Schoolhouse.

RAILROAD *Crossing*

Quilts from the turn of the 20th century fueled designer Cindy Blackberg's color choices for this quilt. A far more recent technique—foundation piecing—ensures accurate seams and sharp points in the arcs. The bright blue background ties together the blocks, each of which is made of a different fabric.

Materials

16—¼-yard pieces of assorted blue prints for blocks

16—¼-yard pieces of assorted light prints for blocks

8—⅛-yard pieces of assorted olive green prints for blocks

12—⅛-yard pieces of assorted cheddar yellow prints for blocks

4—⅛-yard pieces of assorted dull gold prints for blocks

12—⅛-yard pieces of assorted pumpkin prints for blocks

4—⅛-yard pieces of assorted light pumpkin prints for blocks

8—⅛-yard pieces of assorted dark orange prints for blocks

1⅞ yards of bright blue print for blocks

⅓ yard of pumpkin print for inner border

2 yards of black print for outer border and binding

3⅓ yards of backing fabric

59×73" of quilt batting

48 sheets of tracing paper

Finished quilt top: 52¾×67"

Quantities specified for 44/45"-wide, 100% cotton fabrics. All measurements include a ¼" seam allowance. Sew with right sides together unless otherwise stated.

continued

Select the Fabrics

Because she wanted to be true to turn-of-the-century color palettes, Cindy Blackberg included olive and pumpkin colors with the variety of blue and cheddar yellow prints she used for this quilt. As she worked, "it became a game to make every block from a different fabric," she says.

Cut the Fabrics

To make the best use of your fabrics, cut the pieces in the order that follows. To make a template of Pattern B, found on *Pattern Sheet 1*, follow the instructions in Quilter's Schoolhouse, which begins on *page 150*.

Cut the outer border strips lengthwise (parallel to the selvage). These border strip measurements are mathematically correct. You may wish to cut your border strips longer than specified to allow for possible sewing differences.

From *each* assorted blue print, cut:
- 24—1½×2½" rectangles
- 15—2×2½" rectangles

From one assorted blue print, cut:
- 6—2½" squares
- 3—4⅛" squares, cutting each diagonally twice in an X for a total of 12 small side triangles (you'll have 2 leftover triangles)
- 2—2⅜" squares, cutting each in half diagonally for a total of 4 corner triangles

From *each* assorted light print, cut:
- 18—2×2½" rectangles
- 48—1½" squares

From *each* assorted olive green print, cut:
- 1 of Pattern B

From *each* of two olive green prints, cut:
- 1—2½" square

From *each* assorted cheddar yellow print, cut:
- 1 of Pattern B

From *each* of two cheddar yellow prints, cut:
- 1—2½" square

From *each* assorted dull gold print, cut:
- 1 of Pattern B

From *each* of two dull gold prints, cut:
- 1—2½" square

From *each* assorted pumpkin print, cut:
- 1 of Pattern B

From *each* of two pumpkin prints, cut:
- 1—2½" square

From *each* assorted light pumpkin print, cut:
- 1 of Pattern B

From *each* of two light pumpkin prints, cut:
- 1—2½" square

From *each* assorted dark orange print, cut:
- 1 of Pattern B

From *each* of two dark orange prints, cut:
- 1—2½" square

From bright blue print, cut:
- 17—8½" squares
- 4—12⅝" squares, cutting each diagonally twice in an X to make a total of 16 side triangles (you'll have 2 leftover triangles)

From pumpkin print, cut:
- 6—1½×42" strips for inner border

From black print, cut:
- 2—4½×67½" outer border strips
- 2—4½×45¼" outer border strips
- 7—2½×42" binding strips

Make the Foundation Papers

1. With a pencil, trace Pattern A, which is on *Pattern Sheet 1*, onto a sheet of tracing paper, tracing all lines and numbers. Repeat to make a total of six tracings. Place each tracing on top of a stack of seven unmarked sheets of tracing paper. (Freezer paper and typing paper also will work.) Staple each stack together once or twice (see Diagram 1).

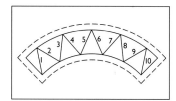

Diagram I

2. Using a sewing machine with an unthreaded, small-gauge needle set on 10 to 12 stitches per inch, sew on each tracing's inside lines through all layers in each paper stack. Do not stitch on the tracings' outer lines.

3. With your scissors, cut each stack on the tracing's outer lines to make a total of 48 perforated foundation papers.

Assemble the Arcs

1. With right sides together, place a light print 2×2½" rectangle atop a blue print 2×2½" rectangle. (Cindy pieced each arc using just two fabrics.) Put a perforated foundation paper on

top of the light print strip, positioning the strips so their right edges are a scant ¼" beyond the first stitching line and so they extend about ⅜" above the top of the arc (see Diagram 2). With the foundation paper on top, sew on stitching line No. 1.

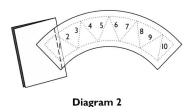

Diagram 2

2. Trim the seam allowance to a scant ¼". (If you're using dark colors, trim the seam allowance so the darker fabric does not show through the lighter fabric.) Press the rectangles open, pressing the seam allowance toward the blue print rectangle. Trim the blue print rectangle to a scant ¼" beyond the next stitching line (see Diagram 3). Trim the pieces even with the top and bottom edges of the foundation paper (see Diagram 4).

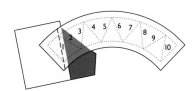

Diagram 3

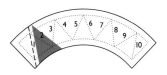

Diagram 4

3. Position a second light print 2×2½" rectangle under the trimmed blue piece with the right edge a scant ¼" beyond the second stitching line. Sew on stitching line No. 2 as before (see Diagram 5).

Trim the seam allowance if needed. Press the pieces open, pressing the seam allowance toward the light print rectangle (see Diagram 6). Trim the second light print rectangle to a scant ¼" beyond the next sewing line. Trim the pieces even with the top and bottom edges of the foundation paper.

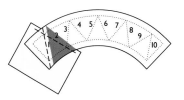

Diagram 5

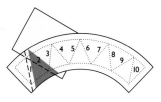

Diagram 6

4. Continue adding blue and light print rectangles to the foundation paper as before until you've pieced the entire arc (see Diagram 7). Then, with the blunt edge of a seam ripper, remove the foundation paper.

Diagram 7

5. Repeat steps 1 through 4 to make a total of 48 pieced arcs.

Assemble the Arc Units

1. With right sides together, pin the center bottom of a pieced arc to the center top of an assorted print B piece (marked with Xs on the patterns). Then pin each end. Pin generously between the ends and the center (see Diagram 8) using slender pins and picking up only a few threads at each position.

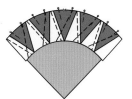

Diagram 8

2. Sew the pieces together either by hand or machine, sewing a little to the right of the sewing line if necessary to ensure sharp points, to make a pieced arc unit.

continued

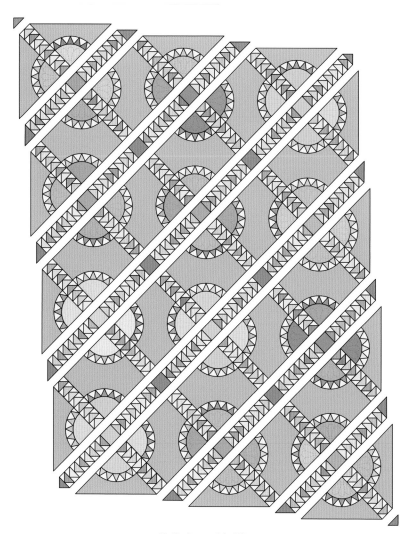

Quilt Assembly Diagram

Assemble the Sashing Units

1. For accurate sewing lines, use a pencil to mark a diagonal line on the wrong side of each light print 1½" square. (To prevent your fabric from stretching as you draw the lines, place 220-grit sandpaper under the squares.)

2. Align a marked light print 1½" square with one end of an assorted blue print 1½×2½" rectangle (see Diagram 9). Stitch on the marked line; trim the seam allowance to ¼". Press the attached triangle open.

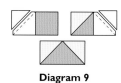

Diagram 9

3. Align a second marked light print 1½" square with the opposite end of the blue print rectangle. Stitch on the marked line; trim and press as before to make a Flying Geese unit.

4. Repeat steps 2 and 3 to make a total of 384 Flying Geese units.

5. Sew together eight Flying Geese units to make a sashing unit (see Diagram 10). Press all the seam allowances in one direction. The pieced sashing unit should measure 2½×8½", including the seam allowances. Repeat to make a total of 48 sashing units.

Diagram 10

Assemble the Quilt Center

1. Referring to the Quilt Assembly Diagram for placement, lay out the 17 bright blue print 8½" squares, 14 bright blue print side triangles, the 48 sashing units, the 18 assorted print 2½" squares for sashing, 10 blue print small side triangles, and four blue print corner triangles. Place a pieced arc unit on each side triangle and two pieced arc units on each square.

2. Once you're pleased with the arrangement, pin each pieced arc unit to its bright blue print triangle or square, aligning straight raw edges.

If you choose to hand-stitch, turn the piece over occasionally to examine the front, checking for a smooth seam.

If you choose to machine-stitch, keep the pieced arc on top when the pieces are under the presser foot. Work slowly, stop the machine often with the needle down, and adjust the direction you're sewing as needed.

Press the seam allowance toward the B piece.

3. Repeat with the remaining pieced arcs and assorted print B pieces to make a total of 48 pieced arc units.

Using thread that matches, appliqué the curved edges of the arc units to the bright blue print backgrounds.

3. Working in diagonal rows, sew together the pieces in each row. Press the seam allowances toward the bright blue print triangles and squares and toward the sashing squares and side triangles. Join the rows, then add the four blue print corner triangles to make the quilt center. Press the seam allowances in one direction. The pieced quilt center should measure 43¼×57½", including seam allowances.

Add the Borders

1. Cut and piece the pumpkin print 1½×42" strips to make the following:
- 2—1½×43¼" inner border strips
- 2—1½×59½" inner border strips

2. Sew the short inner border strips to the top and bottom edges of the pieced quilt center. Then add the long inner border strips to the side edges of the pieced quilt center. Press all seam allowances toward the pumpkin print border.

3. Sew the black print 4½×45¼" outer border strips to the top and bottom edges of the pieced quilt center. Then add the black print 4½×67½" outer border strips to the side edges of the pieced quilt center to complete the quilt top. Press all seam allowances toward the black print border.

Complete the Quilt

1. Layer the quilt top, batting, and backing according to the instructions in Quilter's Schoolhouse, which begins on *page 150*.

2. Quilt as desired. Cindy hand-quilted ¼" inside each arc triangle and ¼" inside each Flying Geese unit. She hand-quilted a floral design inside each Pattern B piece (see design inside Pattern B on *Pattern Sheet 1*) and a 1"-wide grid in the bright blue print squares and triangles. She hand-quilted the border with 1"-wide parallel lines.

3. Use the black print 2½×42" strips to bind the quilt according to the instructions in Quilter's Schoolhouse.

Railroad Crossing Quilt
optional sizes

If you'd like to make this quilt in a size other than for a wall hanging, use the information *below*.

Alternate quilt sizes	Twin	Full/Queen	King
Number of blocks	31	49	84
Number of blocks wide by long	5 rows of 3	6 rows of 4	7 rows of 6
	4 rows of 4	5 rows of 5	6 rows of 7
Finished size	67×81¼"	81¼×95½"	109¾" square
Yardage requirements			
Assorted blue prints	3 yards	3¾ yards	5¾ yards
Assorted light prints	3¼ yards	4¼ yards	6¾ yards
Assorted Pattern B prints	¾ yard	⅞ yard	1½ yards
Bright blue print for block background	2¾ yards	3¾ yards	6½ yards
Pumpkin print for inner border	⅜ yard	½ yard	½ yard
Black print for outer border and binding	2⅜ yards	2⅞ yards	3⅓ yards
Backing	5 yards	7⅓ yards	9⅔ yards
Batting	73×88"	88×102"	116" square

RAILROAD PILLOW

The most prominent patterns in "Railroad

Crossing" are perfect for a pillow.

Materials

⅝ yard of solid black for Flying Geese units, arc units, and piping

¼ yard of solid beige for Flying Geese units and arc units

⅜ yard of solid brown for arc units, pillow sides, and pillow backing

2½" square of solid dark brown for center square

2 yards of ⅛"-diameter cotton cording

10½"-diameter pillow form 2" deep

Finished pillow top: 10" in diameter

Cut the Fabrics

To make the best use of your fabrics, cut the pieces in the order that follows. The project uses "Railroad Crossing" patterns, which are on *Pattern Sheet 1*. To make a template of Pattern B, follow the instructions in Quilter's Schoolhouse, which begins on *page 150*.

Refer to the Make the Foundation Papers instructions on *page 50* to make a total of four perforated foundation papers.

From solid black, cut:
- 20—2×2½" rectangles
- 16—1½×2½" rectangles
- 1—18" square, cutting it into enough 1"-wide bias strips to total two 38"-long pieces, for cording cover (See Cutting Bias Strips in Quilter's Schoolhouse for specific instructions.)

From solid beige, cut:
- 32—1½" squares
- 24—2×2½" rectangles

From solid brown, cut:
- 2—6½×12" rectangles
- 4 of Pattern B
- 1—2⅜×35½" strip

From solid dark brown, cut:
- 1—2½" square

Assemble the Sashing Units

1. Referring to Assemble the Sashing Units on *page 52*, steps 1 through 3, use solid beige 1½" squares and solid black 1½×2½" rectangles to make a total of 16 Flying Geese units.

2. Sew together four Flying Geese units in a row to make a sashing unit (see Diagram 2 on *page 52*). Press all seam allowances in one direction. The pieced sashing unit should measure 2½×4¾", including the seam allowances. Repeat to make a total of four sashing units.

Assemble the Arc Units

1. Referring to Assemble the Arcs and Assemble the Arc Units on *pages 50 and 51*, use the solid black and solid beige 2×2½" rectangles to make a total of four pieced arcs.

2. Add each pieced arc to a solid brown B piece for a total of four arc units.

Assemble the Pillow Top

1. Referring to the photograph at *right* for placement, lay out the arc units, sashing units, and the solid dark brown 2½" square in three horizontal rows. Sew together the pieces in each row. Press the seam allowances away from the sashing units.

2. Sew together the rows to make the pillow top. The pieced pillow top should measure 11" in diameter, including the seam allowances.

Complete the Pillow

1. Machine-baste the solid brown 6½×12" rectangles together along the 12" edges using a ½" seam allowance to make the pillow back. (This is a temporary seam.) Press the seam allowance in one direction.

2. Center the pieced pillow top on the pieced pillow back square. Cut the pieced back to the exact size and shape as the pillow top.

3. With the wrong side inside, fold under 1½" at one end of one solid black 1"-wide bias strip. Fold the strip in half lengthwise with the wrong side inside. Insert the cording next to the folded edge, placing a cording end 1" from the strip's folded end. Using a machine cording foot, sew through both fabric layers right next to the cording. (For more specific instructions on covered cording, see Quilter's Schoolhouse, which begins on *page 150*.)

4. Starting on one side of the pieced pillow top, align the raw edges and stitch the covered cording to the right side of the pillow top. Begin stitching 1½" from the cording's folded end.

5. Once the cording is stitched around the edge of the pillow top, cut the end of the cording so that it will fit snugly into the folded opening at the beginning. The ends of the cording should abut inside the cording cover. Stitch the ends down and trim the raw edges as needed.

6. Repeat steps 3 through 5 to add cording to the prepared pillow back.

7. Sew together the short ends of the solid brown 2⅜×35½" strip to make a continuous pillow side; press the seam allowance in one direction. Sew together the pieced pillow top and the solid brown pillow side with the cording seam allowance between the layers. Repeat to stitch the pillow back to the opposite edge of the pillow side to complete the pillow cover.

8. Open the temporary basted seam of the pillow back using a seam ripper. Turn the pillow cover right side out. Insert the pillow form through the opening. Whipstitch the opening closed to complete the pillow.

PASTEL QUILT

A floral border sets the stage for the palette of pastel Flying Geese that frame the green print squares in this bed quilt. Exquisite quilting emphasizes the angular design.

Materials

2¼ yards of cream pin dot for Flying Geese units and sashing squares

1¾ yards total of assorted pastel prints for Flying Geese units

2¾ yards of green print for blocks and side triangles

¼ yard of small purple floral for sashing squares and side and corner triangles

⅜ yard of cream print for inner border

2⅝ yards of large purple floral for outer border

¾ yard of purple print for binding

5⅓ yards of backing fabric

81×96" of quilt batting

Finished quilt top: 75×89¼"

Cut the Fabrics

To make the best use of your fabrics, cut the pieces in the order that follows.

Cut the outer border strips lengthwise (parallel to the selvage). These border strip measurements are mathematically correct. You may wish to cut your border strips longer than specified to allow for possible sewing differences.

From cream pin dot, cut:
• 1,280—1½" squares
• 20—2½" squares
From assorted pastel prints, cut:
• 640—1½×2½" rectangles
From green print, cut:
• 31—8½" squares
• 5—12⅝" squares, cutting each diagonally twice in an X to make a total of 20 side triangles (you'll have 2 leftover triangles)
From small purple floral, cut:
• 12—2½" squares
• 4—4⅛" squares, cutting each diagonally twice in an X for a total of 16 side triangles (you'll have 2 leftover triangles)
• 2—2⅜" squares, cutting each in half diagonally for a total of 4 corner triangles

From cream print, cut:
- 7—1½×42" strips for inner border

From large purple floral, cut:
- 2—8½×89¾" outer border strips
- 2—8½×59½" outer border strips

From purple print, cut:
- 9—2½×42" binding strips

Assemble the Sashing Units

1. Referring to Assemble the Sashing Units instructions on *page 52*, use cream pin dot 1½" squares and assorted pastel print 1½×2½" rectangles to make a total of 640 Flying Geese units.

2. Use the Flying Geese units to make a total of 80 sashing units.

Assemble the Quilt Center

1. Referring to the photograph at *right* for placement, lay out the 31 green print 8½" squares and 18 green print side triangles. Then place the 80 pieced sashing units between the squares and triangles. Add the 20 cream pin dot 2½" sashing squares, the 12 small purple floral 2½" sashing squares, 14 small purple floral side triangles, and the four small purple floral corner triangles to the layout.

2. Referring to Assemble the Quilt Center, Step 3, on *page 53*, sew together the pieces to make the quilt center. The pieced quilt center should measure 57½×71¾", including the seam allowances.

Add the Borders

1. Cut and piece the cream print 1½×42" strips to make the following:
- 2—1½×71¾" inner border strips
- 2—1½×57½" inner border strips

2. Sew the short inner border strips to the top and bottom edges of the pieced quilt center. Then add the long inner border strips to each side edge of the quilt center. Press all seam allowances toward the inner border.

3. Sew the large purple floral 8½×59½" outer border strips to the top and bottom edges of the pieced quilt center. Then add the large purple floral 8½×89¾" outer border strips to the side edges of the pieced quilt center to complete the quilt top. Press all the seam allowances toward the outer border.

Complete the Quilt

1. Layer the quilt top, batting, and backing according to the instructions in Quilter's Schoolhouse, which begins on *page 150*. Quilt as desired.

2. Use the purple print 2½×42" strips to bind the quilt according to the instructions in Quilter's Schoolhouse.

Apple Core

The plethora of plaids in this wall hanging satisfies designer Sharlene Jorgenson's

passion for this favorite fabric. She cut her selection of plaids into apple core

pieces, then randomly placed them in her quilt top for a homespun look.

Materials

4 yards total of assorted scraps of red and green

plaids, stripes, and checks for apple cores

(minimum scrap size should be 4½×5¼")

1 yard of green plaid for binding

3⅛ yards of backing fabric

56" square of quilt batting

Finished quilt top: 49¾" square

Quantities specified for 44/45"-wide, 100% cotton fabrics. All measurements include a ¼" seam allowance. Sew with right sides together unless otherwise stated.

Select the Fabrics

When she's selecting fabric, Sharlene Jorgenson takes her time. She auditions possibilities by cutting them into pieces, then positioning the pieces puzzle style on a flat surface.

"I play with the fabric," she says. "Then I live with it for a day or two to see if I like it." Only after each fabric passes her test of time is it sewn into her quilt.

"Don't be afraid to eliminate a piece of fabric," she says. "You'll use it later in another scrap project."

For her Apple Core wall hanging, Shar pulled from her considerable collection of plaids. Rather than going for high contrast, she stayed in the middle range between lights and darks. Random placement gives the quilt a casual, scrappy look.

This quilt would look even scrappier if made from crumbs (Shar's word for scraps of fabric left

continued

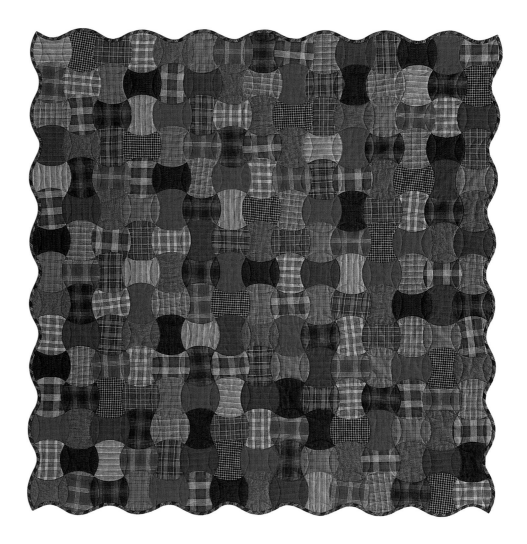

over from other quilt projects). Sew the crumbs together at random; when the piece is a reasonable size, press the seam allowances open. Place an apple core template on top of the pieced fabric and cut the needed pattern pieces.

Cut the Fabrics

When she's working with multiple scraps, Shar cuts as many as six layers of fabric at one time. She uses a 28 mm rotary cutter to assure accuracy of the curved pieces, and a 6×8" or 8×12" rotary mat.

"When I cut plaid, I don't worry if the pattern piece is parallel to the plaid," she says. "The slightly offset patterns add interest to your quilt."

To make the best use of your fabrics, cut the pieces in the order that follows. The pattern is on *Pattern Sheet 1*. To make a template of the pattern, follow the instructions in Quilter's Schoolhouse, which begins on *page 150*.

From assorted red and green plaids, stripes, and checks, cut:
- 225 of Apple Core Pattern

From green plaid, cut:
- 20—2"-wide bias strips for binding (For specific instructions, see Cutting Bias Strips in Quilter's Schoolhouse.)

Assemble the Rows

1. Mark the center of all four edges of the apple core pieces. Shar does this by folding each piece in half both ways and cutting a small notch in each crease mark. Do not cut the notches too deeply as you don't want to cut into the seam allowance. You also can mark the centers with pins or a fabric pencil.

2. If you won't be randomly placing your pieces, lay them out in the desired positions. Working with the first two apple core pieces in the first row, match the center of a convex edge with the

center of a concave edge (see Diagram 1). Place a slender pin, such as extra-fine silk pins, precisely at the center ¼" seam allowance.

Next, place a slender pin at each end of the curve. Picking up only a few threads at a time, continue pinning and easing the fabric between the pins until the pieces fit smoothly together (see Diagram 2).

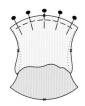

Diagram I **Diagram 2**

3. Sew together the two pieces, removing each pin just before your needle comes to it. Press the seam allowance toward the concave piece.

4. Using the same method, join all the apple core pieces in the first row. Repeat with all 15 rows, alternating the position of the first piece with each row as shown in the photograph *opposite*. Press the seam allowances as indicated in Diagram 3.

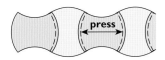

Diagram 3

Assemble the Quilt Top

To join the rows, it works best to sew partial seams as described in the instructions that follow.

1. Begin with the first two rows of the quilt top. Pin together the apple core pieces where a concave piece is on top (see Diagram 4). Sew together the pinned pieces.

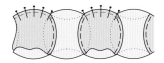

Diagram 4

2. Flip the rows over, and pin them together in the same manner (see Diagram 5). Sew together the pinned pieces. New seams should overlap

previous seams by about four stitches at the beginning and end of each seam.

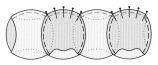

Diagram 5

3. Repeat steps 1 and 2 until you've sewn together all the rows and made the quilt top. Press the seam allowances in one direction.

Complete the Quilt

1. Layer the quilt top, batting, and backing according to the instructions in Quilter's Schoolhouse, which begins on *page 150*.

2. Quilt as desired. Phyllis Peterson machine-quilted the wall hanging shown *opposite*. To use her method, begin stitching between the rows at the start position shown on Diagram 6. Follow the stitching line indicated with red arrows to the opposite edge of the quilt. At the end of the row, turn the quilt around and follow the stitching line back to the start position. Quilt all the rows in this manner.

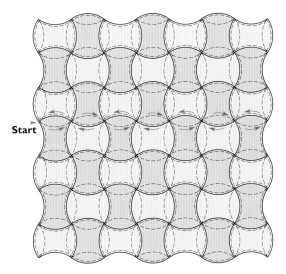

Diagram 6

3. Use the 2"-wide bias strips to bind the quilt according to the instructions in Quilter's Schoolhouse. Do not stretch the bias binding when sewing it around the curves of the quilt. If you stretch it, your quilt will not lie flat, and it may pucker.

continued

Apple Core Quilt
optional sizes

If you'd like to make this quilt in a size other than for a wall hanging, use the information *below*.

Alternate quilt sizes	Twin	Full/Queen	King
Number of blocks	475	725	1,089
Number of blocks wide by long	19×25	25×29	33×33
Finished size	62¾×80¼"	82¼×93¼"	108¼×106¼"
Yardage requirements			
Total of assorted plaids, stripes, and checks	8 yards	12 yards	17¾ yards
Binding	1 yard	1 yard	1 yard
Backing	4⅞ yards	7½ yards	9⅝ yards
Batting	69×87"	89×100"	115" square

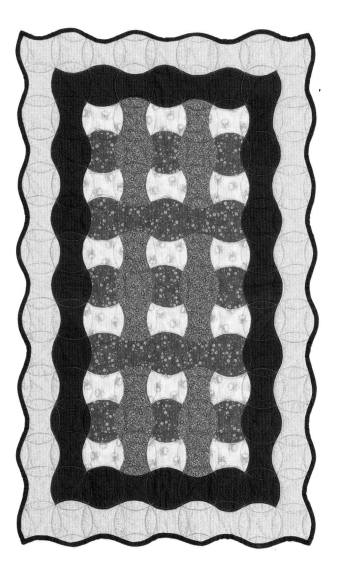

TABLE RUNNER

The carefully planned placement of fabric brings out a basketweave design in this Apple Core table runner.

Materials

⅜ yard of red print for apple cores

⅜ yard of blue print for apple cores

⅜ yard of yellow print No. 1 for apple cores

1¾ yards of dark blue print for apple cores and binding

¾ yard of yellow print No. 2 for apple cores

1½ yards of backing fabric

35×54" of quilt batting

Finished quilt top: 29×48"

Cut the Fabrics

To make the best use of your fabrics, cut the pieces in the order that follows. This project uses the Apple Core Pattern on *Pattern Sheet 1*. To make templates of this pattern, follow the instructions in Quilter's Schoolhouse, which begins on *page 150*.

From red print, cut:
• 19 of Apple Core Pattern
From blue print, cut:
• 18 of Apple Core Pattern
From yellow print No. 1, cut:
• 18 of Apple Core Pattern
From dark blue print, cut:
• 36 of Apple Core Pattern
• 1—18×42" rectangle, cutting it into enough 2"-wide bias strips to total 200" in length (For specific instructions, see Cutting Bias Strips in Quilter's Schoolhouse.)
From yellow print No. 2, cut:
• 44 of Apple Core Pattern

Assemble the Table Runner Top

1. Referring to the photograph *opposite* for color placement, lay out the apple core pieces.

2. Referring to Assemble the Rows on *page 60*, sew together the pieces in each row.

3. Referring to Assemble the Quilt Top on *page 61*, sew the rows together to complete the table runner top.

Complete the Table Runner

1. Layer the table runner top, batting, and backing according to instructions in Quilter's Schoolhouse, which begins on *page 150*. Quilt as desired.

2. Referring to Complete the Quilt on *page 61*, use the dark blue print 2"-wide bias strips to bind the quilt.

SIGNATURE QUILT

Apple core pieces are fused to make the centerpiece of this colorful quilt. Whether it's for a favorite teacher or to mark a special occasion, add signatures and this wall hanging is sure to become a treasured gift.

Materials

1 yard total of assorted bright prints in green, blue, purple, yellow, black, orange, and red for apple cores and binding

¼ yard of light yellow print for apple cores

¾ yard of green-and-yellow plaid for appliqué foundation

⅝ yard of red print for border

1⅛ yards of backing fabric

38" square of quilt batting

1 yard of lightweight fusible web

Machine-embroidery thread in colors to match the quilt top

Permanent fine-line fabric pen (optional)

Finished quilt top: 32" square

Cut the Fabrics

To make the best use of your fabrics, cut the pieces in the order that follows. This project uses the Apple Core Pattern on *Pattern Sheet 1*. To use fusible appliqué, as was done in this project, follow the steps below.

1. Lay the fusible web, paper side up, over the Apple Core Pattern. With a pencil, trace the dashed lines on the pattern 49 times, leaving ½" between tracings. Cut out the fusible-web pieces roughly ¼" outside of the traced lines.

2. Following the manufacturer's instructions, press the fusible-web pieces onto the backs of the apple-core fabrics; you'll need 36 of the assorted bright prints and 13 of the light yellow print. Let the fabrics cool. Cut out the fabric pieces on the drawn lines. Peel off the paper backings.

From green-and-yellow plaid, cut:
• 1—24" square appliqué foundation
From red print, cut:
• 2—4½×32" border strips
• 2—4½×24" border strips

Appliqué the Quilt Center

1. Referring to the photograph *below* for color placement, lay out the apple core pieces on the green-and-yellow plaid 24" square appliqué foundation.

2. When the pieces are correctly positioned, fuse in place with a hot, dry iron; let the fabrics cool.

3. Machine-appliqué the pieces in place to complete the quilt center. The appliquéd quilt center should measure 24" square, including seam allowances.

Add the Border

Sew the red print 4½×24" border strips to the top and bottom edges of the pieced quilt center. Then join the red print 4½×32" border strips to the side edges of the pieced quilt center to complete the quilt top; press.

Complete the Quilt

From assorted bright prints, cut:

- Enough 2½"-wide pieces of varying lengths from 15 to 19" to total 135" in length

1. Layer the quilt top, batting, and backing according to the instructions in Quilter's Schoolhouse, which begins on *page 150*. Quilt as desired.

2. Piece the assorted bright print 2½" pieces into a 135"-long strip. Use it to bind the quilt according to the instructions in Quilter's Schoolhouse.

3. Use the permanent fine-line fabric pen to add signatures to the blocks.

ROTARY-CUT CLASSICS

The rotary cutter revolutionized the art of quilting by reducing the time needed to cut the fabric and making piecing easier with the accurately cut triangles, squares, and rectangles.

Whether your aim is the charm of "Pinwheels and Posies," the vintage appeal of "Hugs and Kisses," or the warmth of "Under the Stars," you'll find your goal is easier reached with rotary-cut pieces.

Try it and see for yourself.

PINWHEELS &
Posies

The pastel prints in this quilt evoke the feeling of a bountiful garden on a warm summer day. Designer Kim Diehl used gold fabrics rather than yellow to cast the glow of late-afternoon sunshine over the surface. Sage green anchors the color scheme.

Materials

1⅞ yards total of assorted ivory prints for blocks

28—⅛-yard pieces of assorted pastel prints for blocks and border

1¾ yards of light tan print for borders

1¼ yards of sage green print for blocks and binding

3⅜ yards of backing fabric

60×66" of quilt batting

Finished quilt top: 54×60"
Finished block: 6" square

Quantities specified for 44/45"-wide, 100% cotton fabrics. All measurements include a ¼" seam allowance. Sew with right sides together unless otherwise stated.

continued

Cut the Fabrics

To make the best use of your fabrics, cut the pieces by section in the order listed.

Cut and Assemble the Pinwheel Blocks

From assorted ivory prints, cut:

- 56—3⅞" squares, cutting each in half diagonally for a total of 112 triangles
- 56—3¼" squares

From *each* of the 28 assorted pastel prints, cut:

- 2—3¼" squares

1. Use a quilter's pencil to draw a diagonal line on the wrong side of the ivory print 3¼" squares. (To prevent the fabric from stretching as you draw the lines, place 220-grit sandpaper under the squares.)

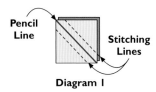

Diagram 1

2. Layer each marked ivory print square atop a pastel print 3¼" square (see Diagram 1). Sew each pair together with two seams, stitching ¼" on either side of the drawn lines.

To save time, designer Kim Diehl chain-pieced the paired squares—machine-sewing them together one after the other without lifting the presser foot or clipping threads between units.

To chain-piece, first sew along one side of the drawn lines (see Diagram 2). Then turn the group of pairs around and sew along the other side of the lines. Clip the connecting threads between the pairs.

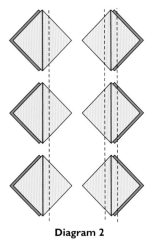

Diagram 2

3. Cut the pairs apart on the drawn lines to make two triangle units each (see Diagram 3). Press each triangle unit open to make a total of 112 triangle-squares (see Diagram 4). Trim corner dog ears; then trim each triangle-square to measure 2⅝" square, including the seam allowances.

Diagram 3   **Diagram 4**

4. Referring to Diagram 5 for placement, lay out four matching triangle-squares in two pairs. Sew together the triangle-squares in each pair. Press the seam allowances in opposite directions. Then join the pairs to make a pinwheel unit. Press the seam allowances in one direction. The pieced pinwheel unit should measure 4¾" square, including the seam allowances.

Diagram 5

5. Sew an ivory print triangle to opposite edges of the pinwheel unit (see Diagram 6). Then join an ivory print triangle to the remaining raw edges of the pinwheel unit to make a Pinwheel block. Press all seam allowances toward the ivory print triangles. The pieced Pinwheel block should measure 6½" square, including the seam allowances.

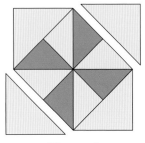

Diagram 6

6. Repeat steps 4 and 5 to make a total of 28 Pinwheel blocks.

Pinwheels & Posies

Cut and Assemble the Posy Blocks

From assorted ivory prints, cut:
- 56—2⅞" squares
- 112—1½×2½" rectangles
- 112—2" squares

From *each* of the 28 assorted pastel prints, cut:
- 1—3⅜" square
- 4—1½" squares

From sage green print, cut:
- 56—¾×4" strips
- 112—2" squares

1. Use a quilter's pencil to draw a diagonal line on the wrong side of the ivory print 2" squares.

2. Layer each marked ivory print square atop a sage green print 2" square. Sew each pair together with two seams, stitching ¼" on either side of the drawn lines.

3. Cut the pairs apart on the drawn lines to make two triangle units each. Press each triangle unit open to make a total of 224 triangle-squares. Trim each triangle-square to measure 1½" square, including the seam allowances.

4. Finger-press under ³⁄₁₆" along the long edges of each sage green print ¾×4" strip to make 56 stem appliqués.

5. Place a prepared sage green print stem diagonally atop an ivory print 2⅞" square (see Diagram 7). Using sage green thread, appliqué the stem in place. Repeat to appliqué each prepared stem atop an ivory print 2⅞" square.

Diagram 7

6. Cut each appliquéd square in half diagonally to make a total of 112 stem triangles (see Diagram 8).

Diagram 8

7. To make a posy block you'll need eight triangle-squares, four stem triangles, four ivory print 1½×2½" rectangles, and one 3⅜" square and four 1½" squares from the same pastel print.

8. Sew a stem triangle to opposite edges of the pastel print 3⅜" square (see Diagram 9). Then join a stem triangle to the remaining raw edges of the pastel print square to make the block center. Press all seam allowances toward the pastel print square. The pieced block center should measure 4½" square, including the seam allowances.

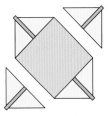

Diagram 9

9. Referring to Diagram 10, lay out the block center and remaining pieces in sections. Join the pieces in each section. Press the seam allowances toward the ivory print 1½×2½" rectangles or pastel print 1½" squares.

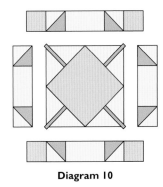

Diagram 10

10. Sew the side sections to the block center. Then add the top and bottom sections to the block center to complete a posy block. Press all seam allowances away from the block center. The pieced posy block should measure 6½" square, including seam allowances.

11. Repeat steps 7 through 10 to make a total of 28 posy blocks.

Assemble the Quilt Center

1. Referring to the photograph on *page 72* for placement, lay out the Pinwheel blocks and posy

continued

From assorted pastel prints, cut:

- 50—4½" squares
- 2—2½" squares

1. Use a quilter's pencil to draw a diagonal line on the wrong side of each light tan print 2½" and 1½" square.

2. Align marked light tan print 2½" squares in opposite corners of a pastel print 4½" square (see Diagram 11); sew on the drawn lines. Trim the seam allowances to ¼", and press the attached triangles open. Then sew a marked light tan print 2½" square to each remaining corner of the pastel print square; trim and press to make a large diamond unit. The large diamond unit should measure 4½" square, including the seam allowances. Press all seam allowances toward the light tan print triangles.

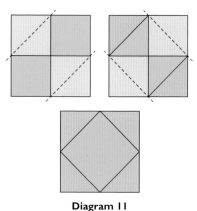

Diagram 11

3. Repeat Step 2 to make a total of 50 large diamond units.

4. Repeat Step 2 using the eight marked light tan print 1½" squares and the two pastel print 2½" squares to make two small diamond units.

5. Aligning long raw edges, sew a light tan print 1½×2½" rectangle to opposite edges of a small diamond unit to make a diamond border unit (see Diagram 12). The diamond border unit should measure 2½×4½", including the seam allowances. Repeat to make a second diamond border unit.

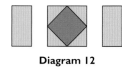

Diagram 12

blocks in eight horizontal rows, alternating blocks. Sew together the blocks in each row. Press the seam allowances toward the Pinwheel blocks.

2. Join the rows to make the quilt center. Press the seam allowances in one direction. The pieced quilt center should measure 42½×48½", including the seam allowances.

Cut and Assemble the Borders

The border strips are cut the length of the fabric (parallel to the selvage). These border strip measurements are mathematically correct. You may wish to cut your strips longer than specified to allow for possible sewing differences.

From light tan print, cut:

- 2—1½×58½" outer border strips
- 2—1½×54½" outer border strips
- 2—1½×48½" inner border strips
- 2—1½×44½" inner border strips
- 200—2½" squares
- 4—1½×2½" rectangles
- 8—1½" squares

6. Sew a light tan print 1½×48½" inner border strip to each side edge of the pieced quilt center. Then add a light tan print 1½×44½" inner border strip to the top and bottom edges of the pieced quilt center. Press all seam allowances toward the light tan print inner border.

7. Referring to the photograph *opposite*, lay out 12 large diamond units and one diamond border unit in a vertical row. Sew together the pieces to make a pieced side border unit. Press the seam allowances in one direction. Repeat to make a second pieced side border unit.

8. Sew the pieced side border units to the side edges of the pieced quilt center. Press the seam allowances toward the light tan print inner border.

9. Join 13 large diamond units to make a pieced top border unit. Repeat to make a pieced bottom border unit. Press all seam allowances in one direction.

10. Sew the pieced top and bottom border units to the top and bottom edges of the pieced quilt center. Press the seam allowances toward the light tan print inner border.

11. Sew a light tan print 1½×58½" outer border strip to each side edge of the pieced quilt center. Then

add a light tan print 1½×54½" outer border strip to the top and bottom edges of the pieced quilt center to complete the quilt top. Press all seam allowances toward the light tan print outer border.

Complete the Quilt

From sage green print, cut:
- 6—2½×42" binding strips

1. Layer the quilt top, batting, and backing according to the instructions in Quilter's Schoolhouse, which begins on *page 150*.

2. Quilt as desired. Kathi Gibson of Idaho Falls, Idaho, free-motion machine-quilted this project. Kathi machine-stippled the background portion of the Pinwheel and posy blocks, outlining the pastel portion of each pinwheel ¼" inside the seam. She quilted the pastel print center of each posy block in a square spiral to give it the look of a flower blossom. Diagonal quilting lines in the border background echo the shape of the pastel print diamonds. Kathi quilted arching lines from point to point in the inside portion of each diamond to round the diamond shape.

3. Use the sage green print 2½×42" strips to bind the quilt according to the instructions in Quilter's Schoolhouse.

optional colors

The background of blues in this wall hanging sets the stage for a brilliant wash of color. The intense contrast between the deep blue background fabrics and almost neon hues makes the pinwheel pattern even more prevalent.

Pinwheels and Posies Quilt
optional sizes

If you'd like to make this quilt in a size other than for a throw, use the information *below*.

Alternate quilt sizes	Wall	Crib	Twin
Number of posy blocks	5	10	66
Number of Pinwheel blocks	4	10	66
Number of blocks wide by long	3×3	4×5	11×12
Number of border diamonds	24	32 + 2 small	74 + 2 small
Finished size	30"	36×42"	78×84"
Yardage requirements			
Assorted ivory prints	½ yard	1 yard	4⅛ yards
Assorted pastel prints	¾ yard	1⅛ yards	3½ yards
Light tan print	1⅛ yards	1½ yards	2⅝ yards
Sage green print	⅝ yard	⅔ yard	1⅞ yards
Backing	1 yard	1⅓ yards	5 yards
Batting	36" square	42×48"	84×90"

MEMO BOARD

The posy block, enlarged and embellished with buttons and ribbon, becomes a memory center for the kitchen, office, or great-room. Select a simple color scheme and add coordinating ribbons and buttons. Favorite photos, today's messages, and reminder notes slip neatly under the ribbons.

Materials

⅛ yard of ivory print for block

¾ yard of yellow print for block and border

4×18" rectangle of red print for block

4¾ yards of red-and-white check ribbon

25½" square of quilt batting

18" square of Homasote or other fiberboard

Staple gun

Glue gun and hotmelt adhesive

8—⅜"-diameter red buttons

Picture hanger

Finished memo board: 18" square

Cut the Fabrics

To make the best use of your fabrics, cut the pieces in the order that follows.

From ivory print, cut:
- 4—1½×2½" rectangles
- 4—2" squares
- 4—1½" squares

From yellow print, cut:
- 2—25½×10" rectangles
- 2—6½×10" rectangles
- 1—3⅜" square

From red print, cut:
- 2—2⅞" squares, cutting each in half diagonally for a total of 4 triangles
- 4—2" squares

From red-and-white check ribbon, cut:
- 8—21"-long strips

Assemble the Memo Board Top

1. Referring to Cut and Assemble the Posy Blocks, on *page 71*, steps 1 through 3, make eight red-and-ivory triangle-squares. Trim each triangle-square to measure 1½" square, including the seam allowances.

2. Sew red print triangles to opposite edges of the yellow print 3⅜" square; add the remaining red print triangles to the square's remaining raw edges to make the block center.

3. Referring to the Block Assembly Diagram, lay out the block center, the eight triangle-squares, the four ivory print 1½×2½" rectangles, and the four ivory print 1½" squares in sections. Join the pieces in each section. Press the seam allowances toward the ivory print squares or rectangles. Then sew together the sections to make a posy block.

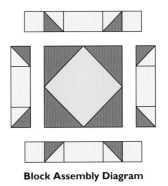

Block Assembly Diagram

4. Sew a yellow print 6½×10" rectangle to opposite edges of the posy block. Then join the yellow print 25½×10" rectangles to the remaining edges of the posy block to complete the memo board top. Press the seam allowances toward the yellow print rectangles. The pieced memo board top should measure 25½" square, including the seam allowances.

Assemble the Memo Board

1. With right sides down, layer the memo board top and batting. Center the fiberboard 18" square atop the layers.

2. Wrap one edge of layers around the board; staple in place, leaving the corners loose. Repeat on the opposite edge, making sure the fabric and batting are smooth and taut. Then wrap and staple on the remaining edges.

3. Trim excess batting to reduce bulk on the back. Gently gather and fold the fabric at each corner; when smooth, staple fabric in place.

4. Staple one end of each ribbon strip to the block (see photograph for placement). Pull the ribbon strips to the back of the board tautly and staple in place.

5. Hot-glue the buttons over the stapled ribbon ends on the message front. Attach a picture hanger to the back of the board.

PINWHEEL QUILT

This wall hanging's Pinwheel blocks of high-, medium-, and low-contrast fabrics capture the imagination. The splashes of color are tempered by the black prints.

Materials

1⅞ yards of black print for blocks

1¾ yards of assorted bright prints for blocks and border

1¾ yards of multicolor print for borders

½ yard of solid black for binding

3⅜ yards of backing fabric

60×66" of quilt batting

Finished quilt top: 54×60"

Cut the Fabrics

To make the best use of your fabrics, cut the pieces by section in the order listed.

Cut and Assemble the Pinwheel Blocks

From black print, cut:
- 112—3⅞" squares, cutting each in half diagonally for a total of 124 triangles
- 36—3¼" squares

From assorted bright prints, cut:
- 188—3¼" squares

Referring to Cut and Assemble the Pinwheel Blocks on *page 70*, make a total of 18 of Pinwheel block A (see Diagram 1). Referring to the same instructions, make a total of 38 of Pinwheel block B (see Diagram 2).

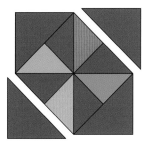
Diagram 1
Pinwheel Block A

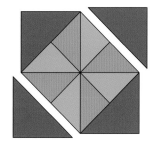
Diagram 2
Pinwheel Block B

Assemble the Quilt Center

1. Referring to the photograph *right* for placement, lay out the 56 Pinwheel blocks in eight horizontal rows, alternating blocks. Sew together the blocks in each row. Press the seam allowances in one direction, alternating the direction with each row.

2. Join the rows to make the quilt center. Press the seam allowances in one direction. The pieced quilt center should measure 42½×48½", including the seam allowances.

Cut and Assemble the Borders

Cut the border strips the length of the fabric (parallel to the selvage). These border strip measurements are mathematically correct. You may wish to cut your strips longer than specified to allow for possible sewing differences.

From multicolor print, cut:
- 2—1½×58½" outer border strips
- 2—1½×54½" outer border strips
- 2—1½×48½" inner border strips
- 2—1½×44½" inner border strips
- 200—2½" squares
- 4—1½×2½" rectangles
- 8—1½" squares

From assorted bright prints, cut:
- 50—4½" squares
- 2—2½" squares

Referring to Cut and Assemble the Borders on *page 72,* piece four border units and add the multicolor print inner border strip, the pieced border units, and the multicolor print outer border strips to the pieced quilt center to complete the quilt top.

Complete the Quilt

From solid black, cut:
- 6—2½×42" binding strips

1. Layer the quilt top, batting, and backing according to the instructions in Quilter's Schoolhouse, which begins on *page 150.* Quilt as desired.

2. Use the solid black 2½×42" strips to bind the quilt according to the instructions in Quilter's Schoolhouse.

HUGS AND *Kisses*

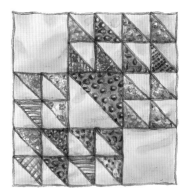

Reproduction prints in a variety of soft blues echo the look of the 1930s in this

charming design from Darlene Zimmerman. Extraordinary quilting on the

sunshine yellow fabric, a hallmark of that same era, enhances the vintage

appeal. Re-create this look with reproduction fabrics in blue and yellow

or use fabrics in your own favorite colors to send a message of love.

Materials

5 yards of solid yellow for blocks, borders,
   and binding

10—¼-yard pieces of assorted blue prints for
   blocks and border

⅜ yard of one blue print for block centers

5 yards of backing fabric

66×90" of quilt batting

Finished quilt top: 60×84"
Finished block: 12" square

Quantities specified for 44/45"-wide, 100% cotton
fabrics. All measurements include a ¼" seam
allowance. Sew with right sides together unless
otherwise stated.

continued

Assemble the Blocks

1. Sew together one solid yellow small triangle and one blue print small triangle to make a small triangle-square (see Diagram 1). Press the seam allowance toward the blue print triangle. The pieced triangle-square should measure 2½" square, including the seam allowances. Repeat to make a total of 704 small triangle-squares.

Diagram 1

2. Sew together one solid yellow large triangle and one blue print large triangle to make a large triangle-square. Press the seam allowance toward the blue triangle. The pieced triangle-square should measure 4½" square, including the seam allowances. Repeat to make a total of 24 large triangle-squares.

3. Referring to Diagram 2 for placement, lay out one large triangle-square, 24 small triangle-squares, and two solid yellow 4½" squares in three horizontal rows.

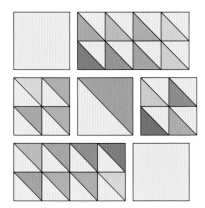

Diagram 2

4. Sew together the pieces in each section. Press the seam allowances toward either the yellow 4½" squares or the large triangle-squares. Then join the sections to make a block. Press the seam allowances in one direction. The pieced block should measure 12½" square, including the seam allowances.

5. Repeat steps 3 and 4 to make a total of 24 pieced blocks.

Cut the Fabrics

To make the best use of your fabrics, cut the pieces in the order that follows.

From solid yellow, cut:
- 23—2½×42" strips for borders and binding
- 12—4⅞" squares, cutting each in half diagonally for a total of 24 large triangles
- 48—4½" squares
- 352—2⅞" squares, cutting each in half diagonally for a total of 704 small triangles
- 4—2½" squares

From assorted blue prints, cut:
- 352—2⅞" squares, cutting each in half diagonally for a total of 704 small triangles

From one blue print, cut:
- 12—4⅞" squares, cutting each in half diagonally for a total of 24 large triangles

Assemble the Quilt Center

1. Referring to the photograph *opposite* for placement, lay out the pieced blocks in six horizontal rows. Sew together the blocks in each row. Press the seam allowances in one direction, alternating the direction with each row.

2. Join the rows to make the quilt center. Press the seam allowances in one direction. The pieced quilt center should measure 48½×72½", including the seam allowances.

Assemble and Add the Borders

1. Cut and piece the solid yellow 2½×42" strips to make the following:
- 2—2½×76½" inner border strips
- 2—2½×48½" inner border strips
- 2—2½×84½" outer border strips
- 2—2½×56½" outer border strips

2. Sew a short solid yellow inner border strip to the top and bottom edges of the pieced quilt center. Then join the long solid yellow inner border strips to the side edges of the pieced quilt center. Press all seam allowances toward the yellow inner border.

3. Referring to the photograph, lay out 26 small triangle-squares in a horizontal row. Sew together the triangle-squares to make a 2½×52½" pieced border strip. Press the seam allowances in one direction. Repeat to make a second 2½×52½" pieced border strip. Join the border strips to the top and bottom edges of the pieced quilt center.

4. Lay out 38 small triangle-squares in a vertical row, adding a solid yellow 2½" square to each end. Sew together the pieces to make a 2½×80½" pieced border strip. Press the seam allowances in one direction. Repeat to make a second 2½×80½" pieced border strip. Join the border strips to the side edges of the pieced quilt center.

5. Sew the short solid yellow outer border strips to the top and bottom edges of the pieced quilt center. Then join the long solid yellow outer border strips to the side edges of the pieced quilt center to complete the quilt top. Press all seam allowances toward the yellow outer border.

Complete the Quilt Top

1. Layer the quilt top, batting, and backing according to the instructions in Quilter's Schoolhouse, which begins on *page 150*. Quilt as desired.

2. Use the remaining solid yellow 2½×42" strips to bind the quilt according to the instructions in Quilter's Schoolhouse.

Hugs and Kisses Quilt
optional sizes

If you'd like to make this quilt in a size other than for a twin bed, use the information *below*.

Alternate quilt sizes	Wall	Full/Queen	King
Number of blocks	4	48	64
Number of blocks wide by long	2×2	6×8	8×8
Finished size	36" square	84×108"	108" square
Yardage requirements			
Solid yellow	2 yards	8½ yards	10¾ yards
Assorted blue prints	¾ yard	4 yards	5¼ yards
Blue print	¼ yard	⅞ yard	1⅛ yards
Backing	1¼ yards	7½ yards	9½ yards
Batting	42"	90×114"	114" square

continued

optional colors

Cheerful colors wave across the sky-blue background in this wall hanging. When placing her fabrics, quilt tester Laura Boehnke followed the rainbow: violet, blue, green, yellow, orange, and red.

The border ties the color scheme together by combining the darkest hues of the blue background with hints of the violet from the center triangle-squares.

REDWORK

Brilliant red prints fade from the outside in,

allowing the eye to linger on the charming

center block bouquet.

Materials

4½×18" piece of white print for blocks

½ yard total of assorted red prints for blocks

½ yard total of assorted white-and-red prints

    for blocks

4½×18" piece of dark red print for blocks

¼ yard of red print for binding

⅞ yard of backing fabric

30" square of quilt batting

Red embroidery floss

Red fine-tip permanent marking pen

Finished quilt top: 24" square

Cut the Fabrics

Carefully review the photograph *opposite* before cutting. Note that the small triangles are shaded from light to dark, from the center out.

To make the best use of your fabrics, cut the pieces in the order that follows.

From white print, cut:
- 4—4½" squares

From assorted red prints, cut:
- 2—4⅞" squares, cutting each in half diagonally for a total of 4 large triangles
- 48—2⅞" squares, cutting each in half diagonally for a total of 96 small triangles

From assorted white-and-red prints, cut:
- 2—4⅞" squares, cutting each in half diagonally for a total of 4 large triangles
- 48—2⅞" squares, cutting each in half diagonally for a total of 96 small triangles

From dark red print, cut:
- 4—4½" squares

From red print, cut:
- 3—2½×42" binding strips

Assemble the Blocks

1. Referring to Assemble the Blocks on *page 80*, use the assorted red print small triangles and assorted white-and-red print small triangles to make a total of 96 small triangle-squares.

2. Use the assorted red print large triangles and assorted white-and-red print large triangles to make a total of four large triangle-squares.

3. Use 24 small triangle-squares, one large triangle-square, one white print 4½" square, and one dark red 4½" square to make a pieced block. Repeat to make a total of four identical pieced blocks.

Assemble the Quilt Top

1. Referring to the photograph at *right* for placement, sew together the four blocks in pairs. Press the seam allowances in opposite directions.

2. Join the pairs to make the quilt top. Press the seam allowance in one direction.

Embroider the Quilt Center

1. Trace the redwork design on *Pattern Sheet 1* on the quilt top using a red fine-tip permanent marking pen.

2. Using a stem stitch and two strands of red embroidery floss, embroider the design.

To stem-stitch, refer to the diagram *below*. First, pull your needle up at A. Insert your needle into the fabric at B, about ⅜" away from A. Holding the floss out of the way, bring your needle back up at C and pull the floss through so it lies flat against the fabric. The distances between points A, B, and C should be equal. Pull with equal tautness after each stitch.

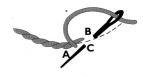

Stem Stitch

3. Using two strands of red embroidery floss, add a French knot to the center of each flower.

To make a French knot, refer to the diagram at *right*. Pull the floss through at the point where the knot is desired (A). Wrap the floss around your needle two times. Insert the tip of the needle into the fabric at B, 1/16" away from A. Gently push the wraps down the needle to meet the fabric. Pull the needle so the floss trails through the fabric slowly and smoothly.

Complete the Quilt

1. Layer the quilt top, batting, and backing according to the instructions in Quilter's Schoolhouse, which begins on *page 150*. Quilt as desired.

2. Use the red print 2½×42" strips to bind the quilt according to the instructions in Quilter's Schoolhouse.

French Knot

LODGE THROW

This quilt features deep, rich, earth-tone

colors that are offset by beiges and tans.

A scrappy tone is set by using a variety

of fabrics.

Materials

3⅛ yards of assorted dark green, dark rust,
  and black plaids, prints, and stripes for blocks
  and borders

2½ yards of assorted beige plaids, prints, and
  stripes for blocks and borders

1⅛ yards of assorted green, brown, and
  tan plaids, prints, and stripes for blocks
  and borders

⅝ yard of green print for binding

3⅞ yards of backing fabric

70×82" of quilt batting

Finished quilt top: 64×76"

Cut the Fabrics

To make the best use of your fabrics, cut the pieces
in the order that follows.

From assorted dark plaids, prints, and stripes, cut:
- 20—4⅞" squares, cutting each in half diagonally
  for a total of 40 large triangles
- 40—4½" squares
- 300—2⅞" squares, cutting each in half diagonally
  for a total of 600 small triangles

From assorted beige plaids, prints, and stripes, cut:
- 56—2½×4½" rectangles
- 300—2⅞" squares, cutting each in half diagonally
  for a total of 600 small triangles

From assorted green, brown, and tan plaids, prints,
and stripes, cut:
- 32—4½×8½" rectangles
- 2—4½" squares

From green print, cut:
- 8—2½×42" binding strips

Assemble the Blocks

1. Referring to Assemble the Blocks on *page 80*,
   use the assorted dark plaid small triangles and
   assorted beige plaid small triangles to make a
   total of 600 small triangle-squares.

2. Use the assorted dark plaid large triangles and the assorted beige plaid large triangles to make a total of 20 large triangle-squares.

3. Use 24 small triangle-squares, one large triangle-square, and two dark plaid 4½" squares to make a pieced block. Repeat to make a total of 20 pieced blocks.

Assemble the Quilt Center

Referring to the photograph *below right* for placement and the Assemble the Quilt Center instructions on *page 81*, lay out the 20 blocks in five horizontal rows and sew together the quilt center. The pieced quilt center should measure 48½×60½", including the seam allowances.

Assemble and Add the Borders

1. Sew together the beige plaid 2½×4½" rectangles end to end to make the following:
- 2—2½×64½" inner border strips
- 2—2½×48½" inner border strips

2. Sew the short inner border strips to the top and bottom edges of the pieced quilt center. Then join the long inner border strips to the side edges of the pieced quilt center. Press all seam allowances toward the inner border.

3. Referring to the photograph at *right,* lay out 26 small triangle-squares in a horizontal row; sew together to make a 2½×52½" pieced border strip. Repeat to make a second 2½×52½" pieced border strip. Join the border strips to the top and bottom edges of the pieced quilt center. Lay out 34 small triangle-squares in a horizontal row; sew together to make a 2½×68½" pieced border strip. Repeat to make a second 2½×68½" pieced border strip. Join the border strips to the side edges of the pieced quilt center.

4. Sew together the green, brown, and tan plaid 4½×8½" rectangles end to end to make the following:
- 2—4½×72½" outer border strips
- 2—4½×56½" outer border strips

5. Sew the short outer border strips to the top and bottom edges of the pieced quilt center. Then add a green, brown, or tan plaid 4½" square to one end of each long outer border strip. Join the pieced outer border strips to the side edges of the pieced quilt center to complete the quilt top.

Complete the Quilt

1. Layer the quilt top, batting, and backing according to the instructions in Quilter's Schoolhouse, which begins on *page 150*. Quilt as desired.

2. Use the green print 2½×42" strips to bind the quilt according to the instructions in Quilter's Schoolhouse.

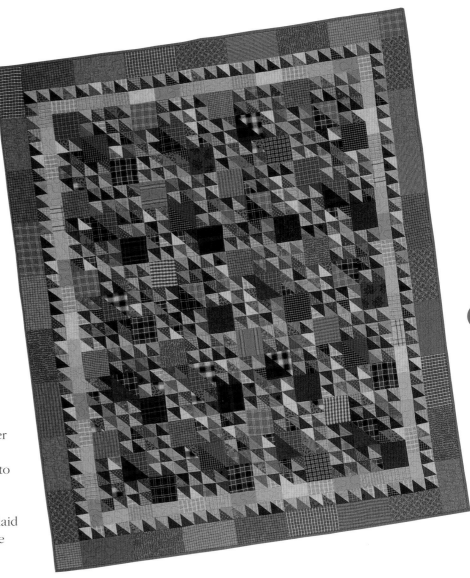

Traditional Log Cabin blocks appliquéd with glowing golden stars result in a spectacular holiday heirloom. Designer Jill Kemp added an embroidered childhood verse for a quilt that warms the heart.

UNDER THE *Stars*

Materials

¼ yard of green print for blocks

12—⅛-yard pieces of assorted red prints for blocks

12—⅛-yard pieces of assorted green prints for blocks

⅛ yard of gold print No. I for star appliqués

⅜ yard of gold print No. 2 for star appliqués and inner border

⅔ yard of dark green print for outer border

½ yard of dark red print for binding

2⅜ yards of backing fabric

57" square of quilt batting

Gold embroidery floss

Finished quilt top: 51" square
Finished block: 10½" square

Quantities specified for 44/45"-wide, 100% cotton fabrics. All measurements include a ¼" seam allowance. Sew with right sides together unless otherwise stated.

continued

From gold print No. 2, cut:
• 5—1½×42" strips for inner border

From dark green print, cut:
• 5—4×42" strips for outer border

From dark red print, cut:
• 6—2½×42" binding strips

Assemble the Log Cabin Blocks

1. Align a red print position 1 strip with the right-hand edge of a green print 3" square (see Diagram 1). Join the pieces. Press the seam allowance toward the red print strip.

Diagram 1

2. Referring to Diagram 2, add a red print position 2 strip to the bottom edge of the pieced Step 1 unit. (Project designer Jill Kemp used strips of the same fabric consecutively.) Press the seam allowance toward the added strip.

Diagram 2

3. Referring to Diagram 3, add a green print position 3 strip to the left-hand edge of the pieced Step 2 unit. Press as before. Then add a green print position 4 strip to the top edge of the pieced unit; press.

Diagram 3

4. Continue adding red and green strips in the numerical sequence indicated in Diagram 4 to make a Log Cabin block. Always press the seam allowances toward the outside. The pieced Log Cabin block should measure 11" square, including the seam allowances.

Cut the Fabrics

To make the best use of your fabrics, cut the pieces in the order that follows.

From green print, cut:
• 16—3" squares

From assorted red prints, cut:
• 16—1½×10" strips for position 14
• 16—1½×9" strips for position 13
• 16—1½×8" strips for position 10
• 16—1½×7" strips for position 9
• 16—1½×6" strips for position 6
• 16—1½×5" strips for position 5
• 16—1½×4" strips for position 2
• 16—1½×3" strips for position 1

From assorted green prints, cut:
• 16—1½×11" strips for position 16
• 16—1½×10" strips for position 15
• 16—1½×9" strips for position 12
• 16—1½×8" strips for position 11
• 16—1½×7" strips for position 8
• 16—1½×6" strips for position 7
• 16—1½×5" strips for position 4
• 16—1½×4" strips for position 3

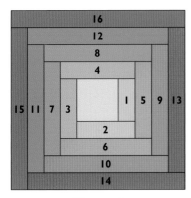

Diagram 4

5. Repeat steps 1 through 4 to make a total of 16 Log Cabin blocks.

Assemble the Quilt Center

1. Referring to the photograph *opposite*, lay out the 16 pieced Log Cabin blocks in four rows, rotating the color placement of each block. Sew together the blocks in each row. Press the seam allowances in one direction, alternating the direction with each row.

2. Join the rows to make the quilt center. Press the seam allowances in one direction. The pieced quilt center should measure 42½" square, including the seam allowances.

Appliqué the Quilt Center

1. The star patterns are on *Pattern Sheet 2*. To make templates of the patterns, follow the instructions in Quilter's Schoolhouse, which begins on *page 150*. To use needle-turn appliqué, as was done for this project, add a ³⁄₁₆" seam allowance when cutting out the appliqué pieces.

From gold print No. 1, cut:
- 3 of Pattern A
- 2 *each* of patterns B and C

From gold print No. 2, cut:
- 3 *each* of patterns A, B, and C

2. Using gold thread, hand-appliqué a star to the center of each Log Cabin block.

Add the Borders

1. Cut and piece the gold print No. 2 1½×42" strips to make the following:
- 2—1½×44½" inner border strips
- 2—1½×42½" inner border strips

2. Sew the short gold print inner border strips to opposite edges of the pieced quilt center. Then add the long gold print inner border strips to the remaining edges of the pieced quilt center. Press all seam allowances toward the gold print border.

3. Cut and piece the dark green print 4×42" strips to make the following:
- 2—4×51½" outer border strips
- 2—4×44½" outer border strips

4. Sew the short dark green print outer border strips to opposite edges of the pieced quilt center. Then add the long dark green print outer border strips to the remaining edges of the pieced quilt center to complete the quilt top. Press all seam allowances toward the dark green print border.

Embroider the Quilt Top

1. Using a chalk pencil and noting placement in the photograph *opposite*, mark the child's wish that follows on the dark green print border. Jill gave the lettering a primitive look by varying slightly the size of the letters and by not stitching in a straight line.

Star light, star bright,
First star I see tonight,
I wish I may, I wish I might,
Have the wish I wish tonight.

2. Using two strands of gold embroidery floss, straight-stitch the marked words.

Complete the Quilt

1. Layer the quilt top, batting, and backing according to the instructions in Quilter's Schoolhouse, which begins on *page 150*. Quilt as desired.

2. Use the dark red print 2½×42" strips to bind the quilt according to the instructions in Quilter's Schoolhouse.

continued

Under the Stars Quilt
optional sizes

If you'd like to make this quilt in a size other than for a wall hanging, use the information *below*.

Alternate quilt sizes	Twin	Full/Queen	King
Number of blocks	35	56	81
Number of blocks wide by long	5×7	7×8	9×9
Finished size	61½×82½"	82½×93"	103½" square
Yardage requirements			
Green print	⅓ yard	½ yard	⅝ yard
Assorted red prints	1¼ yards	3¼ yards	3½ yards
Assorted green prints	2¼ yards	3¾ yards	5¼ yards
Gold print No. 1	⅓ yard	½ yard	⅝ yard
Gold print No. 2	⅝ yard	¾ yard	1 yard
Dark green print	1 yard	1⅛ yards	1⅓ yards
Binding	⅝ yard	⅔ yard	⅞ yard
Backing	5 yards	7½ yards	9¼ yards
Batting	68×89"	89×99"	110" square

EMBROIDERED PILLOW

Stars of gold burst from the deep blue background of this pillow.

Materials

¼ yard of blue print for pillow top

⅞ yard of gold print for star appliqués and

pillow back

⅓ yard total of assorted light to medium prints

for pillow top

20" pillow form

Gold embroidery floss

Scraps of fusible web

Finished pillow: 20" square

Cut the Fabrics

To make the best use of your fabrics, cut the pieces in the order that follows.

To use fusible web for appliquéing, as was done in this project, use the following steps.

1. Lay the fusible web, paper side up, over "Under the Stars" patterns A and B on *Pattern Sheet 2*. With a pencil, trace each pattern twice, leaving ½" between tracings. Cut out the pieces roughly ¼" outside the traced lines.

2. Following the manufacturer's instructions, press the fusible-web shapes onto the back of the gold print; let cool. Cut out the pieces on the drawn lines. Peel off the paper backings.

From blue print, cut:
• 1—8½" square
• 4—6½" squares

From gold print, cut:
- 2—20½×25" rectangles for pillow back

From assorted light to medium prints, cut:
- 36—1½×6½" strips

Assemble the Pillow Top

1. Aligning long edges, join nine assorted print 1½×6½" strips. Press the seam allowances in one direction. Trim the strip set to measure 6½×8½", including the seam allowances, to make a pieced unit. Repeat to make a total of four pieced units.

2. Referring to the photograph *above*, sew a pieced unit to opposite edges of the blue print 8½" square. Press the seam allowances toward the blue print square.

3. Add a blue print 6½" square to each end of the remaining pieced units and press the seam allowances toward the blue print squares. Sew these pieced units to the remaining edges of the Step 2 unit to complete the pillow top; press the seam allowances open. The pieced pillow top should measure 20½" square, including the seam allowances.

4. Position the prepared appliqué pieces on the pieced pillow top; fuse in place.

Embroider the Pillow Top

1. Referring to Embroider the Quilt Top on *page 89,* mark and stitch the stars and words on the pillow top.

2. Using two strands of gold embroidery floss, blanket-stitch around each fused star. (For blanket-stitch instructions, see *page 131.*)

Complete the Pillow

1. With wrong sides inside, fold each gold print 20½×25" rectangle in half to form two double-thick 12½×20½" pieces. Overlap the folded edges by 4". Stitch ¼" from the top and bottom edges, including across the folds, to secure the pieces, and create the pillow back.

2. With right sides together, layer the pillow top and the pillow back. Sew the pieces together along all four edges; turn right side out. Insert the pillow form through the back opening.

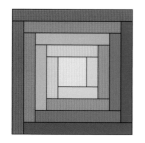 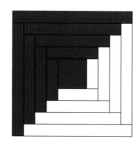 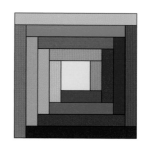 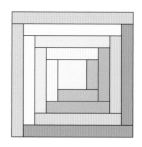

LOG CABIN INSPIRATION

The popular Log Cabin block is simple enough for a beginner

and has so many setting variations that it has held the interest

of experienced quilters for generations.

The success of Log Cabin quilt designs depends on a strong contrast between the fabrics on either side of the diagonal that forms when the strips, or "logs," are pieced into a block. The setting or placement of the individual blocks in a quilt top creates a multitude of looks (at *right* and *opposite*).

Most often Log Cabin blocks are scrappy—made with a multitude of fabrics. For a dramatic look, choose two high-contrast colors, such as red and green, or light and dark variations of the same color, such as lavender and plum.

Traditionally, Log Cabin blocks were made with a red center square, which represented the hearth in the log cabin home. Today's quilters use a variety of colors for the center square; the choice may or may not match the light or dark fabrics used in the rest of the block.

Barn Raising Set, *right*
In this setting the placement of lights and darks creates a pattern that radiates from the center of the quilt.

These Log Cabin blocks are made with a light-color center square, red prints on one side of the block, and green prints on the opposite side. In both cases, the red and green prints graduate from lighter shades near the center to darker shades on the outside.

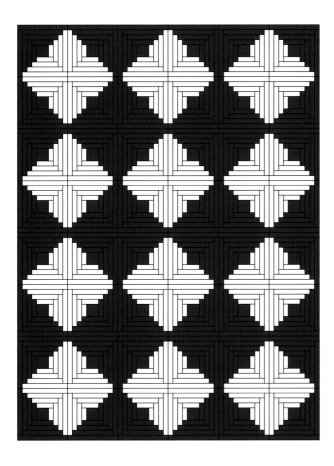

Light and Dark Set, *left*

A pattern of blocks on point emerges in this setting where the Log Cabin blocks are rotated so lights and darks meet.

To make this work, select only two high-contrast fabrics—blue and white in this case—or choose many prints in just two colors, keeping the values similar within each color.

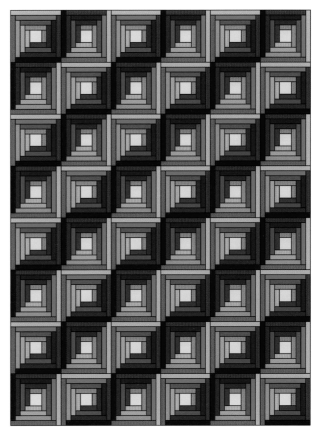

Straight Furrow Set, *above*

Diagonal bands of color move across the quilt top in this setting.

To re-create the version illustrated, use light to medium prints on one side of each Log Cabin block and medium to dark prints on the opposite side.

Streaks of Lightning Set, *left*

Vertical zigzags running the length of the quilt result from the rotating placement of lights and darks in this setting.

Assorted white prints form one side of each Log Cabin block and assorted pastel prints compose the other side.

BRIGHT DELIGHTS

This trio of cheerful projects will delight even your most serious side and give you an opportunity to stretch your creativity as a quilter.

A bountiful garden, a riot of color, and a rooster proudly strutting all celebrate life with vivid clarity. Pick one to make for yourself or as a gift. Then feature a favorite motif in a new way, experiment with unfamiliar colors, or try a technique that's new to you.

As your quilt expands, so will your skill.

SOMETHING TO
Crow About

The folk art rooster looks as if it just stepped off the weather vane onto

designer Sandy Bonsib's homey wall hanging, which is based on the

traditional Nine-Patch block. She used eight prints and plaids in

various color combinations for a scrappy look.

Materials

8—½-yard pieces of assorted purple, navy, gold, and red plaids and prints for blocks and border

¼ yard *each* of dark red print and dark blue print for binding

18×22" piece (fat quarter) of black print for rooster appliqué

2⅜ yards of backing fabric

47×57" of quilt batting

Black perle cotton

Finished quilt top: 41½×50½"
Finished block: 9" square

Quantities specified for 44/45"-wide, 100% cotton fabrics. All measurements include a ¼" seam allowance. Sew with right sides together unless otherwise stated.

Designer Notes

For one of her eight ½-yard pieces, designer Sandy Bonsib chose a bright novelty print as the focal point of this quilt. The seven additional fabrics chosen, both prints and plaids, coordinate with the colors in the umbrellas.

Sandy appliquéd the rooster onto her quilt after it was quilted; she used needle-turn appliqué. The rooster can also be appliquéd to the quilt top before quilting using a machine or hand blanket stitch.

continued

Cut and Assemble the Nine-Patch-in-a-Square Blocks

Pair the remaining purple, navy, gold, and red plaids and prints to create six fabric sets. (Individual fabrics will be used in more than one set.)

Use the following cutting and piecing instructions for each of your six fabric sets to make a total of 24 Nine-Patch-in-a-Square blocks. The four extra blocks will allow you to experiment with different quilt center layouts.

For instructional purposes, a navy print and gold print set was used.

From *each* fabric in the set, cut:
- 3—2½×16" strips
- 4—6" squares, cutting each in half diagonally for a total of 8 triangles

1. Aligning long edges, sew two navy print 2½×16" strips to a gold print 2½×16" strip to make a strip set A (see Diagram 1). Press the seam allowances toward the gold print strip. Cut the strip set into six 2½"-wide segments.

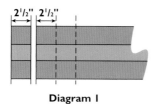

Diagram 1

2. In the same manner, sew two gold print 2½×16" strips to a navy print 2½×16" strip to make strip set B (see Diagram 2). Press the seam allowances toward the gold print strips. Cut the strip set into six 2½"-wide segments.

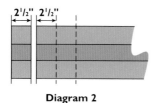

Diagram 2

3. Referring to Diagram 3, sew together two strip set A segments and one strip set B segment to make a Nine-Patch unit A. Press the seam allowances in one direction. Pieced Nine-Patch unit A should measure 6½" square, including seam allowances. Repeat to make a second Nine-Patch unit A.

Cut the Fabrics

To make the best use of your fabrics, cut the pieces in the order that follows. To make a template of the pattern found on *Pattern Sheet 2*, follow the instructions in Quilter's Schoolhouse, which begins on *page 150*.

From *each* of six assorted purple, navy, gold, and red plaids and prints, cut:
- 3—1½×42" strips

From *each* of three assorted purple, navy, gold, and red plaids and prints, cut:
- 1—1½×42" strip

From dark red print, cut:
- 5—2×21" binding strips

From dark blue print, cut:
- 5—2×21" binding strips

4. Repeat Step 3 using two strip set B segments and one strip set A segment to make a Nine-Patch unit B (see Diagram 4). Press the seam allowances in one direction. Pieced Nine-Patch unit B should measure 6½" square, including seam allowances. Repeat to make a second Nine-Patch unit B.

Diagram 3   **Diagram 4**

5. Sew a gold print triangle to opposite edges of a Nine-Patch unit A (see Diagram 5). Press the seam allowances toward the gold print triangles. Then sew a gold print triangle to the remaining raw edges of the unit to complete the Nine-Patch-in-a-Square block. Trim the pieced block to measure 9½" square, including seam allowances.

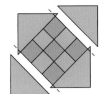

Diagram 5

6. Repeat Step 5, sewing four navy print triangles to the remaining Nine-Patch unit A, four gold print triangles to one Nine-Patch unit B, and four navy print triangles to the remaining Nine-Patch unit B to make a total of four Nine-Patch-in-a-Square blocks (see Diagram 6).

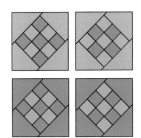

Diagram 6

Assemble the Quilt Center

1. Referring to the photograph *opposite*, lay out 20 Nine-Patch-in-a-Square blocks in five horizontal rows. (You'll have four leftover blocks.) When pleased with the arrangement, sew them together in rows. Press the seam allowances in one direction, alternating the direction with each row.

2. Join the rows to complete the quilt center. Press the seam allowances in one direction. The pieced quilt center should measure 36½×45½", including the seam allowances.

Assemble and Add the Borders

The border strips for this project are made longer than necessary. Before adding the border strip to the appropriate side edge, measure the same edge of your quilt center. Trim the pieced border strip to fit. Then sew the border strip to the quilt center; press the seam allowance toward the quilt center.

1. Aligning long edges, sew together six assorted plaid and print 1½×42" strips to make a border unit A strip set (see Diagram 7). Press the seam allowances in one direction. Repeat to make a total of three border unit A strip sets. Cut the strip sets into 3¼"-wide segments for a total of 25 border unit A segments.

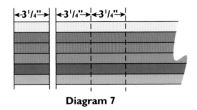

Diagram 7

2. In the same manner, sew together the three assorted plaid and print 1½×42" strips to make a border unit B strip set. Press the seam allowances in one direction. Cut the strip set into 3¼"-wide segments for a total of 11 border unit B segments.

3. Sew together eight border unit A segments to make the left edge border strip. Measure and trim as previously described. Join the strip to the left edge of the quilt center; press the seam allowance toward the quilt center.

4. Sew together seven border unit A segments to make the top border strip. Measure and trim as previously described. Sew the top border strip to the quilt center; press the seam allowance toward the quilt center.

5. Sew together six border unit A segments and four border unit B segments to make the right edge border strip. Sandy rotated the border unit B segments to add interest (see Diagram 8 *on page 100*). Measure and trim as previously described.

continued

Sew the right edge border strip to the quilt center; press the seam allowance toward the quilt center.

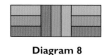

Diagram 8

6. Sew together four border unit A segments and seven border unit B segments to make the bottom border strip. Sandy again rotated the border unit B segments. Measure and trim as previously described. Sew the bottom border strip to the quilt center to complete the quilt top; press the seam allowance toward the quilt center.

Complete the Quilt

1. Layer the quilt top, batting, and backing according to the instructions in Quilter's Schoolhouse, which begins on *page 150*. Quilt as desired.

2. Sew together the five dark red print and five dark blue print 2×21" strips end to end, alternating colors, to make a binding strip. Use the pieced binding strip to bind the quilt according to the instructions in Quilter's Schoolhouse.

Appliqué the Rooster
From black print, cut:
• 1 of Rooster Appliqué Pattern (leave a ³⁄₁₆" seam allowance on the outer edge; do not cut into the tail section)

1. Finger-press the seam allowance under. Referring to the photograph on *page 98* for placement, baste the rooster appliqué to the finished quilt. Using small slip stitches and black thread, appliqué the outer edges of the rooster in place.

Cut away the inner appliqué areas a small portion at a time (2" to 3"), cutting a scant ⅛" from the drawn lines. Appliqué the raw edges in place, using the drawn lines as a guide for turning under the seam allowances with your needle. When turning under tight inside curves, clip the seam allowance up to the drawn line.

2. Using the black perle cotton and running stitches, hand-stitch a wing shape on the rooster's side.

Something to Crow About Quilt
optional sizes

If you'd like to make this quilt in a size other than for a throw, use the information *below*.

Alternate quilt sizes	Twin	Full/Queen	King
Number of blocks	54	90	121
Number of blocks wide by long	6×9	9×10	11×11
Finished size	59½×86½"	86½×95½"	104½" square
Yardage requirements			
Assorted plaids and prints	5½ yards	8⅝ yards	11¼ yards
Black print	18×22"	18×22"	18×22"
Binding	½ yard	⅝ yard	⅔ yard
Backing	5¼ yards	7¾ yards	9¼ yards
Batting	66×93"	93×102"	111" square

CURTAIN

Frame a favorite print with a strip-pieced border for a quick and unique curtain.

Materials

4 yards of light yellow print for curtain panel

1¼ yards total of assorted blue prints for block
    and strip borders

⅜ yard total of assorted yellow prints for
    block border

1 yard total of assorted green prints for strip border

4⅜ yards of cream print for backing and sleeve

Finished curtain: 72×80"

Cut the Fabrics

To make the best use of your fabrics, cut the pieces in the order that follows.

From light yellow print, cut:
- 1—40½×70½" rectangle
- 1—24½×70½" rectangle

From assorted blue prints, cut:
- 21—1½×42" strips
- 6 sets of five 2½" squares
- 6 sets of four 2½" squares

From assorted yellow prints, cut:
- 6 sets of five 2½" squares
- 6 sets of four 2½" squares

From assorted green prints, cut:
- 21—1½×42" strips

Assemble the Center Panel

Aligning long edges, join the two light yellow print rectangles to make a 64½×70½" curtain panel.

Assemble and Add the Border

1. Referring to Diagram 4 on *page 99*, lay out one set of four blue print 2½" squares and one set of five yellow print 2½" squares in three vertical rows. Sew together the squares in each row. Press the seam allowances toward the blue print squares. Then join the rows to make a Nine-Patch block. Press the seam allowances in one direction. Repeat to make a total of six Nine-Patch blocks.

2. Referring to Diagram 3 on *page 99*, lay out one set of four yellow print 2½" squares and one set of five blue print 2½" squares in three vertical rows. Sew together the squares in each row. Press the seam allowances toward the blue print squares. Then join the rows to make a Nine-Patch block. Press the seam allowances in one direction. Repeat to make a total of six Nine-Patch blocks.

3. Referring to Assemble and Add the Borders on *page 99*, Step 1, join six assorted blue print and green print strips to make a strip set. Repeat to make a total of five strip sets. Cut the strip sets into a total of sixty 4½"-wide segments.

4. Cut and piece the 4½"-wide segments to make the following:
- 1—4½×72½" border strip
- 2—4½×70½" border strips

5. Sew the short pieced border strips to the side edges of the curtain panel. Then join the long pieced border strip to the bottom edge of the curtain panel. Press all seam allowances toward the curtain panel.

continued

6. Sew together the 12 Nine-Patch blocks to make a row. Press the seam allowances in one direction. Join the row to the top edge of the curtain panel to complete the curtain front.

Complete the Curtain

1. With right sides together, layer the curtain front and backing. Sew together the layers, leaving a 10" opening along one edge for turning. Turn the curtain right side out; press. Slip-stitch the opening closed. Topstitch ¼" from all edges.

2. Using the remaining cream print fabric, add a hanging sleeve for a rod pocket to the back top edge to complete the curtain. For specific instructions on making a hanging sleeve, see Quilter's Schoolhouse, which begins on *page 150.*

TOILE QUILT

Set the Nine-Patch-in-a-Square block on

point to showcase an elegant toile print.

Finished quilt: 79¾×92½"

Cut the Fabrics

To make the best use of your fabrics, cut the pieces in the order that follows.

From assorted dark prints, cut:
- 34 sets of four 2½" squares

From assorted light prints, cut:
- 34 sets of five 2½" squares

From navy print, cut:
- 9—6½×42" strips for outer border
- 60—6" squares, cutting each in half diagonally for a total of 120 triangles

From blue print, cut:
- 8—2½×42" strips for inner border
- 40—6" squares, cutting each in half diagonally for a total of 80 triangles

From toile print, cut:
- 5—14" squares, cutting each diagonally twice in an X for a total of 20 setting triangles (you'll have 2 leftover triangles)
- 2—7¼" squares, cutting each in half diagonally for a total of 4 corner triangles
- 20—6½" squares

From dark blue print, cut:
- 9—2½×42" binding strips

Cut and Assemble the Nine-Patch-in-a-Square Blocks

1. Referring to Diagram 4 on *page 99,* lay out one set of four dark print 2½" squares and one set of five light print 2½" squares. Sew together the squares in each row. Press the seam allowances toward the dark print squares. Then join the rows to make a Nine-Patch unit. Press the seam allowances in one direction.

2. Repeat Step 1 to make a total of 34 Nine-Patch units. Set aside four units for the outer border.

3. Referring to Cut and Assemble the Nine-Patch-in-a-Square Blocks on *page 99*, Step 5, add four navy print triangles to 30 Nine-Patch units to make a total of 30 Nine-Patch-in-a-Square blocks.

4. In the same manner, add four blue print triangles to each edge of a toile print 6½" square to make a setting block. Trim the pieced block to measure 9½" square, including the seam allowances. Repeat to make a total of 20 setting blocks.

Assemble the Quilt Center

1. Referring to the photograph *opposite* for placement, lay out the blocks and toile print setting triangles in diagonal rows. If the toile print is directional, make sure all of the toile squares within the setting blocks are positioned the same.

2. Sew together the pieces in each row. Press the seam allowances toward the setting blocks and setting triangles. Then join the rows. Press the seam allowances in one direction. Add the toile print corner triangles to complete the quilt center. The pieced quilt center should measure 64¼×77", including the seam allowances.

Add the Borders

1. Cut and piece the blue print 2½×42" strips to make the following:
   • 2—2½×81" inner border strips
   • 2—2½×64¼" inner border strips

2. Sew the short inner border strips to the top and bottom edges of the quilt center. Then add the long inner border strips to the side edges of the quilt center. Press all seam allowances toward the inner border.

3. Cut and piece the navy print 6½×42" strips to make the following:
   • 2—6½×93" outer border strips
   • 2—6½×68¼" outer border strips

4. Sew the short outer border strips to the top and bottom edges of the quilt center. Then add a Nine-Patch unit to each end of the long outer border strips. Add these pieced outer border strips to the side edges of the quilt center to complete the quilt top. Press all seam allowances toward the outer border.

Complete the Quilt

1. Layer the quilt top, batting, and backing according to the instructions in Quilter's Schoolhouse, which begins on *page 150*. Quilt as desired.

2. Use the dark blue print 2½×42" strips to bind the quilt according to the instructions in Quilter's Schoolhouse.

Let this cheerful assortment of pieced and appliquéd produce reflect your healthy outlook on life. Gardening with her young son inspired designer Stephanie Martin Glennon's novel wall hanging.

NOAH'S *Garden*

Materials

For corn row:

⅛ yard *each* of prints in yellow, tan, light green, dark green, and green

⅛ yard of solid blue

For pepper row:

8—4" squares of solids shading from light yellow to orange

Scrap of solid light green

32½×4½" strip of solid dark green

For carrot row:

¼ yard of brown print

⅛ yard of light green print

⅛ yard of orange print

For tomato row:

8—4" squares of solids shading from light red to dark red

32½×4½" strip of solid lime green

For radish row:

¼ yard of burgundy print

¼ yard of green print

¼ yard of red stripe

For finishing:

1⅜ yards of light green print for border

1½ yards of green geometric print for border

⅛ yard of red print for appliqués

⅜ yard of solid green for binding

2 yards of backing fabric

46×50" of quilt batting

Green embroidery floss

Finished quilt top: 39×43½"

Quantities specified for 44/45"-wide, 100% cotton fabrics. All measurements include a ¼" seam allowance. Sew with right sides together unless otherwise stated.

continued

Cut and Assemble the Vegetable Rows

To make the best use of your fabrics, cut the pieces in the order listed in each of the following sections. The patterns are on *Pattern Sheet 2.* To make templates, follow the instructions in Quilter's Schoolhouse, which begins on *page 150.*

To use needle-turn appliqué, as was done in this project, add a ³⁄₁₆" seam allowance to all edges when cutting out the appliqué pieces.

Corn

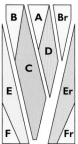

From yellow print, cut:
- 8 of Pattern A

From tan print, cut:
- 8 of Pattern D

From light green print, cut:
- 8 of Pattern E

From dark green print, cut:
- 8 of Pattern E reversed

From green print, cut:
- 8 of Pattern C

From solid blue, cut:
- 8 *each* of patterns B, B reversed, F, and F reversed

1. For one corn unit you'll need one of each pattern piece. Referring to Diagram 1, lay out the pieces. Sew together the pieces in sections as shown. Then join the sections to make a corn unit (see Diagram 2). The pieced corn unit should measure 4½×9½", including the seam allowances. Repeat to make a total of eight corn units.

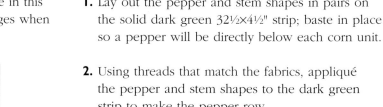

Diagram 1 **Diagram 2**

2. Sew together the eight corn units to make the corn row. The pieced corn row should measure 32½×9½", including the seam allowances.

Peppers

From *each* 4" square shading from light yellow to orange, cut:
- 1 of Pattern G

From solid light green scrap, cut:
- 8 of Pattern H

1. Lay out the pepper and stem shapes in pairs on the solid dark green 32½×4½" strip; baste in place so a pepper will be directly below each corn unit.

2. Using threads that match the fabrics, appliqué the pepper and stem shapes to the dark green strip to make the pepper row.

Carrots

From brown print, cut:
- 1 *each* of patterns M and M reversed
- 7 *each* of patterns O and L
- 1 *each* of patterns I and I reversed
- 8 of Pattern K

From light green print, cut:
- 8 *each* of patterns J and J reversed

From orange print, cut:
- 8 of Pattern N

1. Lay out the pieces for the carrot top row (see Diagram 3). Sew together the pieces in sections as shown. Then join the sections to make a row. The pieced carrot top row should measure 32½×4¼", including the seam allowances.

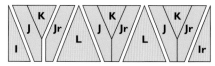

Diagram 3

2. Lay out the pieces for the carrot bottom row (see Diagram 4). Sew together the pieces in sections as shown. Then join the sections to make a row. The pieced carrot bottom row should measure 32½×6¼", including the seam allowances.

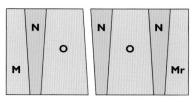

Diagram 4

3. Join the carrot top and bottom rows to make the carrot row. Press the seam allowance toward the carrot bottom row. The pieced carrot row should measure 32½×10", including the seam allowances.

Tomatoes

From *each* 4" square shading from light red to dark red, cut:

• 1 of Pattern P

1. Lay out the tomato shapes on the solid lime green 32½×4½" strip; baste or pin in place. With thread that matches the fabric, appliqué the shapes to the lime green strip to make the tomato row.

2. Using two strands of green embroidery floss, embroider three lazy daisy stitches on the top of each tomato for stems.

To make a lazy daisy stitch, pull your needle up at A and form a loop of floss on the fabric surface. Holding the loop in place, insert your needle back into the fabric at B, about ¹⁄₁₆" away from A. Bring the needle tip out at C and cross it over the trailing floss, keeping the floss as flat as possible. Gently pull the needle and trailing floss until the loop lies flat against the fabric. Push the needle through to the back at D to secure the loop in place.

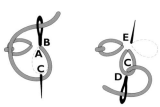

Lazy Daisy Stitch

Radishes

From burgundy print, cut:
• 1—32½×4½" strip
• 1 *each* of patterns Q and Q reversed
• 7 of Pattern S
From green print, cut:
• 8 of Pattern R
From red stripe, cut:
• 8 of Pattern T

1. Lay out the pieces for the radish top row (see Diagram 5). Sew together the pieces in sections as shown. Then join the sections to make a row.

The pieced radish top row should measure 32½×6½", including the seam allowances.

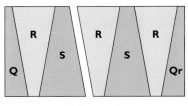

Diagram 5

2. Lay out the radish shapes on the burgundy print 32½×4½" strip; baste or pin in place. With thread that matches the fabric, appliqué the radish pieces to the burgundy strip to make the radish bottom row.

3. Join the radish top and bottom rows to make the radish row. Press the seam allowance toward the top row. The pieced radish row should measure 32½×10½", including seam allowances.

Assemble the Quilt Center

Referring to the photograph on *page 108*, lay out the vegetable rows. Sew together the rows to make the quilt center. Press the seam allowances in one direction. The pieced quilt center should measure 32½×37", including the seam allowances.

Cut, Assemble, and Add the Border

Cut the border strips lengthwise (parallel to the selvage).

From light green print, cut:
• 2—2×48" border strips
• 2—2×44½" border strips
From green geometric print, cut:
• 2—4×53" border strips
• 2—4×48" border strips
From red print, cut:
• 24 of Pattern U

1. Fold the light green print border strips in half lengthwise; finger-press and unfold. Align the center fold of the Appliqué Border Pattern on *Pattern Sheet 2* with the center of a light green print border strip. Moving the pattern along the strip, trace the scalloped edge; cut along the scalloped edge, adding a ³⁄₁₆" seam allowance. Repeat with the remaining light green print border strips. Turn under the seam allowance on each strip's scalloped edge; baste.

Noah's Garden

continued

2. With right sides up and midpoints aligned, match the straight raw edges of each scalloped border strip with a green geometric print border strip; baste. Using light green thread, appliqué the scalloped edges in place, leaving 2" free at each end, to make appliquéd border strips.

3. With midpoints aligned, sew the short appliquéd border strips to the top and bottom edges of the quilt center and the long appliquéd border strips to the side edges of the quilt center, mitering the corners with basting stitches. (For information on mitering corners, see the Mitered Border Corner instructions in Quilter's Schoolhouse.) Check to make sure the scalloped edges meet at each corner; adjust, if necessary, and baste in place. Remove the miter basting and appliqué the loose scalloped edges in place. Miter each corner to complete the quilt top.

4. Using thread that matches the fabric, appliqué the cherry tomato shapes to the border.

5. Using two strands of green embroidery floss, embroider four lazy daisy stitches on each cherry tomato for stems. (Refer to the instructions and diagram on *page 107*.)

Complete the Quilt
From solid green, cut:
- 5—2½×42" binding strips

1. Layer the quilt top, batting, and backing according to the instructions in Quilter's Schoolhouse, which begins on *page 150*. Quilt as desired.

2. Use the solid green 2½×42" binding strips to bind the quilt according to the instructions in Quilter's Schoolhouse.

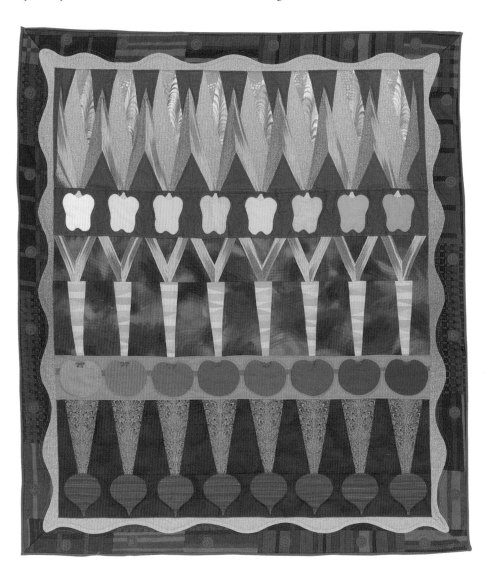

RADISH TOTE

A row of radishes transforms this shopping

bag into a tote with personality. It's easy

to do with fusible web.

Materials

Scraps of green prints for appliqués

Scraps of red prints for appliqués

Purchased tote bag

Heavyweight fusible web

Cut the Fabrics

To make the best use of your fabrics, cut the pieces in the order that follows.

To use fusible web for appliquéing, as was done in this project, use the following steps.

1. Lay the fusible web, paper side up, over "Noah's Garden" patterns R and T on *Pattern Sheet 2*. With a pencil, trace each pattern three times, leaving ½" between tracings. Cut out the pieces roughly ¼" outside the traced lines.

2. Following the manufacturer's instructions, press the fusible-web shapes onto the back of the designated fabrics; let cool. Cut out the pieces on the drawn lines. Peel off the paper backings.

From assorted green prints, cut:
• 3 of Pattern R
From assorted red prints, cut:
• 3 of Pattern T

3. Position the prepared appliqué pieces on the tote bag; fuse in place.

CARROT COVERALLS

Plant a trio of appliquéd carrots along

the legs of a busy toddler's coveralls.

Materials

Scrap of green print for appliqués

Scrap of orange print for appliqués

Purchased children's denim overalls with

   snap crotch

Lightweight fusible web

Machine embroidery thread in matching colors

Cut the Fabrics

To make the best use of your fabrics, cut the pieces in the order that follows.

To use fusible web for appliquéing, as was done in this project, use the following steps.

1. Lay the fusible web, paper side up, over "Noah's Garden" patterns V and W on *Pattern Sheet 2*. With a pencil, trace each pattern three times, leaving ½" between tracings. Cut out the pieces roughly ¼" outside the traced lines.

2. Following the manufacturer's instructions, press the fusible-web shapes onto the back of the designated fabrics; let cool. Cut out the pieces on the drawn lines. Peel off the paper backings.

From green print scrap, cut:
• 3 of Pattern V

From orange print scrap, cut:
• 3 of Pattern W

3. Position the prepared pieces on the denim coveralls; fuse in place.

4. Using color-coordinated embroidery threads, machine-satin-stitch the pieces in place.

TABLE LINENS

Set a summer table with crisp linens

garnished with cheery cherry tomatoes.

Materials

Scraps of solid red for tomato appliqués

⅓ yard of green print for vine appliqué

Green embroidery floss

70"-diameter white tablecloth

4 dinner napkins

Lightweight fusible web

Machine embroidery thread in matching colors

Cut the Fabrics

To make the best use of your fabrics, cut the pieces in the order that follows.

To use fusible web for appliquéing, as was done in this project, use the following steps.

1. Lay the fusible web, paper side up, over "Noah's Garden" Pattern U on *Pattern Sheet 2*. With a pencil, trace the pattern 34 times, leaving ½" between tracings. Cut out the pieces roughly ¼" outside the traced lines.

2. Following the manufacturer's instructions, press the fusible-web shapes onto the back of the solid red fabric; let cool. Cut out the pieces on the drawn lines. Peel off the paper backings.

From green print, cut:

- 2—12" squares, cutting them into enough 1½"-wide bias strips to total 240" in length (For specific instructions on cutting bias strips, see Quilter's Schoolhouse, which begins on *page 150*.)

3. Fold each green print 1½"-wide bias strip in half lengthwise with the wrong side inside and press.

4. Sew the long edges of each folded strip together. Trim each seam allowance to ⅛". Roll each seam allowance to the center of its strip; press the seam allowance to one side so that neither the seam nor the seam allowance is visible along the edges.

5. Position the prepared vine along the edge of the tablecloth, between 3" and 7" from the outer edge of the tablecloth. Baste in place. Machine-appliqué the vine in place.

6. Position the solid red circles along either side of the stitched vine; fuse in place. Fuse each remaining solid red circle to a napkin corner.

7. Machine-satin-stitch around the edges of all the solid red circles.

8. Using two strands of green embroidery floss and lazy daisy stitches, add four stitches to the center of each solid red circle to make a cherry tomato. (Refer to the instructions and diagram on *page 107*.)

RAZZLE
Dazzle

An unconventional construction method

leaves raw edges exposed in Jill Abeloe Mead's quilt

of hand-dyed solid brights, geometric prints,

and solid black flannel.

Materials

4½ yards of solid black flannel for blocks
   and binding

8—18×22" pieces (fat quarters) of assorted
   hand-dyed solid brights for blocks

8—18×22" pieces (fat quarters) of assorted black-
   and-white prints for blocks

44" square of quilt batting

Basting spray (optional)

Finished quilt top: 46" square
Finished block: 5¾" square

Quantities specified for 44/45"-wide, 100% cotton
fabrics. All measurements include a ¼" seam
allowance.

Designer Notes

The exposed raw edges add a touch of surprise
to this bold quilt. Designer Jill Mead's fast and
unconventional construction method involves
stuffing individual blocks with batting, and then
sewing them together, leaving the unfinished seam
allowances on the quilt top surface. She used a
basting spray, rather than pins, to hold the fabrics
in place as she assembled the blocks.

continued

Cut the Fabrics

To make the best use of your fabrics, cut the pieces in the order that follows.

From solid black flannel, cut:
- 5—2½×42" binding strips
- 16—12½" squares
- 64—6¼" backing squares

From *each* of eight assorted solid brights, cut:
- 1—10" square
- 1—8" square
- 2—6" squares

From *each* of eight assorted black-and-white prints, cut:
- 1—10" square
- 1—8" square

From quilt batting, cut:
- 64—5½" squares

Assemble the Units

1. Fold a solid black flannel 12½" square in half diagonally twice and finger-press the folded edges; unfold the square. In the same manner, fold and finger-press a solid bright 10" square, a black-and-white print 8" square, and a solid bright 6" square; unfold. Lightly spray the wrong side of the 10", 8", and 6" squares with basting spray.

2. Center the solid bright 10" square atop the solid black 12½" square with right sides up; use the creased lines as positioning guides. Using black thread, machine-stitch ¼" inside the solid bright 10" square's raw edges (see Diagram 1).

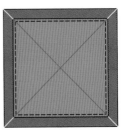 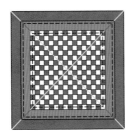

Diagram 1   **Diagram 2**

3. Center the black-and-white 8" square atop the solid bright 10" square with right sides up; machine-stitch the black-and-white 8" square in place as before, sewing through all layers (see Diagram 2).

4. Center the solid bright 6" square atop the black-and-white 8" square with right sides up; sew in place as before (see Diagram 3).

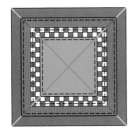

Diagram 3

5. Beginning at the upper left-hand corner of the 10" square, use black thread to machine-stitch in a random zigzag pattern through all layers to complete a unit A (see Diagram 4).

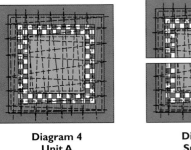 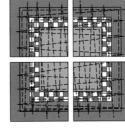

Diagram 4   **Diagram 5**
Unit A   **Subunit A**

6. Repeat steps 1 through 5 to make a total of eight of unit A.

7. Cut each unit A into four 6¼" squares to make a total of 32 A subunits (see Diagram 5).

8. Repeat steps 1 through 5 using the remaining solid black flannel 12½" squares, the black-and-white print 10" squares, the solid bright 8" squares, and the remaining solid bright 6" squares to make a total of eight of unit B (see Diagram 6). Cut each unit B into four 6¼" squares to make a total of 32 B subunits (see Diagram 7).

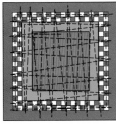 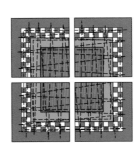

Diagram 6   **Diagram 7**
Unit B   **Subunit B**

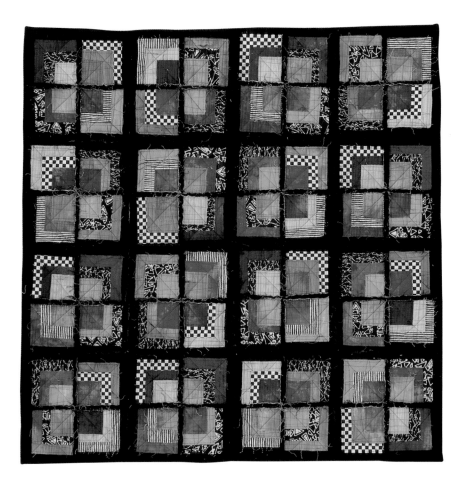

Assemble the Blocks

1. Sandwich a quilt batting 5½" square centered between the wrong sides of an A subunit and a solid black flannel 6¼" square. Baste the layers.

2. Using black thread, machine-stitch diagonally twice through all layers, backstitching to secure the thread ends, to make a "stuffed" block (see Diagram 8).

Diagram 8

3. Repeat steps 1 and 2 with each remaining A subunit and B subunit to make a total of 64 "stuffed" blocks.

Assemble the Quilt

1. Referring to the photograph *above* for placement, lay out the 64 blocks in eight rows, alternating A and B subunits.

2. With the back sides of the blocks together, join the blocks in each row. Backstitch to secure the thread at all seam ends. Press open the seam allowances, which are on the quilt top's right side.

3. With the back sides of the rows together, join the rows to make the quilt. Backstitch to secure the thread at all seam ends. Press the seam allowances open.

    Note: If any batting shifts during assembly and becomes visible from the right side, either trim it away or color it with a permanent black marker.

Complete the Quilt

1. Use the solid black 2½×42" strips to bind the quilt according to the instructions in Quilter's Schoolhouse, which begins on *page 150*.

2. Using a gentle soap, machine-wash the quilt, then machine-dry it. Remove it from the dryer, take the quilt outdoors, and shake it well. The raw edges of the quilt will "bloom" in the washing and drying. Trim frayed thread ends as desired.

continued

optional sizes

If you'd like to make this quilt in a size other than for a wall hanging, use the information *below*.

Alternate quilt sizes	Crib	Twin	Full/Queen
Number of blocks	48	192	288
Number of blocks wide by long	6×8	12×16	16×18
Finished size	34½×46"	69×92"	92×103½"
Yardage requirements			
Solid black flannel	3½ yards	12 yards	17¾ yards
Assorted hand-dyed solid brights	1½ yards	4½ yards	6½ yards
Assorted black-and-white prints	1¼ yards	3½ yards	4¾ yards
Batting	40" square	81×96"	92×108"

WALL HANGING

Setting the blocks on point draws out a layered look in this wall quilt combining deep colors with tone-on-tone prints in an array of hues.

Materials

1½ yards total of assorted olive, plum, gold, brown, and tan prints for blocks

¼ yard of black print for binding

1⅛ yards of backing fabric

31×39" of quilt batting

2½ yards of lightweight fusible web

Finished quilt top: 24⅜×32½"

Cut the Fabrics

To make the best use of your fabrics, cut the pieces in the order that follows.

To use fusible web for appliquéing, as was done in this project, use the following steps.

1. On the fusible web, trace eight 10" squares, eight 8" squares, and eight 6" squares, leaving ½" between tracings. Cut out the pieces roughly ¼" outside of the traced lines. To reduce bulk in the finished project, cut ¼" inside the drawn lines, and remove the center.

2. Following the manufacturer's instructions, press the fusible-web squares onto the backs of assorted olive, plum, gold, brown, and tan prints; let cool. Cut out the pieces on the drawn lines. Peel off the paper backings.

3. Cut each fused square into four equal squares of 5", 4", or 3".

4. From assorted olive, plum, gold, brown, and tan prints, cut:
   • 32—6¼" squares

5. Referring to the Block Assembly Diagram, layer a 5" square, a 4" square, and a 3" square atop an assorted print 6¼" square; align the unfused raw edges on two sides and fuse in place. Repeat with the remaining squares.

Block Assembly Diagram

6. Using a short stitch length, machine-satin-stitch over each inside raw edge to complete a block.

7. Repeat steps 5 and 6 to make a total of 32 blocks.

Assemble the Quilt Top

1. Referring to the photograph *above right* for placement, lay out the 32 blocks in diagonal rows. The blocks used at the corners and along the sides will be trimmed later.

2. Sew together the blocks in each row. Press the seam allowances in one direction, alternating the direction with each row. Then join the rows to make the quilt center.

3. Trim the quilt center to measure 24⅞×33", leaving ¼" beyond the corners of interior blocks.

Machine-satin-stitch across all remaining seams to complete the quilt top.

Complete the Quilt
From black print, cut:
• 3—2½×42" binding strips

1. Layer the quilt top, batting, and backing according to instructions in Quilter's Schoolhouse, which begins on *page 150*. Quilt as desired.

2. Use the black print 2½×42" strips to bind the quilt according to instructions in Quilter's Schoolhouse.

HOMESPUN PILLOW

Earth-tone plaids, buttery yellows, and rich reds give this pillow a scrappy, homespun look. Raw edges emphasize the aura of livable folk art.

Materials

2 yards total of assorted red, black, gold, and
     tan plaids for blocks

1⅓ yards of black plaid for backing

24" square pillow form

Finished pillow: 24" square

Cut the Fabrics

From assorted red, black, gold, and tan plaids, cut:

- 4—12½" squares
- 4—10" squares
- 4—8" squares
- 16—6¼" squares
- 4—6" squares

From black plaid, cut:

- 2—23½×28" rectangles

Assemble the Units

Referring to Assemble the Units on *page 114*, make a total of 16 subunits.

Assemble the Blocks

Referring to Assemble the Blocks on *page 115*, make a total of 16 "stuffed" blocks.

Assemble the Pillow Top

Referring to Assemble the Quilt on *page 115* and the photograph *opposite*, sew together the 16 stuffed blocks in four horizontal rows to make the pillow top. The pieced top should measure 23½" square, including seam allowances.

Complete the Pillow

I. With wrong sides inside, fold each black plaid 23½×28" rectangle in half to form two double-thick 14×23½" pieces. Overlap the folded edges by 5". Stitch ¼" from the top and bottom edges, including across the folds, to secure the pieces and create the pillow back.

2. Layer the pillow top and the pillow back. Sew the pieces together along all four edges; turn right side out. Insert the pillow form through the back opening.

GIFT BAG

Take a few minutes to embellish your next gift bag. Adorned with fabrics in the recipient's favorite colors, it's sure to be an instant hit.

Materials

Scraps of fabric for appliqués

Scraps of heavyweight fusible web

Paper gift bag

Cut the Fabrics

To use fusible web for appliquéing, as was done in this project, use the following steps.

I. On the fusible web, trace one 2¾" square, one 3¾" square, and one 4¾" square, leaving ½" between tracings. Cut out the pieces directly on the traced lines.

2. Following the manufacturer's instructions, press the fusible-web squares onto the backs of assorted print scraps; let cool. Cut out the pieces, cutting along the edge of the fusible web on two adjacent sides, and adding ½" from the fusible web edge on the remaining two adjacent edges.

3. Snip the unfused edges of each square with a scissors to create fringe.

4. Layer the squares on the gift bag, aligning raw edges on two sides; fuse in place, using a pressing cloth to protect the paper gift bag.

5. Use fabric scraps to tie a bow on the bag's handle.

ARTFUL APPLIQUÉ

The traditional look of appliqué can be achieved using a variety of methods, whether stitching by hand or by machine.

Explore this creative art through "Scrap Apple," "Antique Peony," and "Butterfly Garden." Your repertoire will expand to include traditional projects, contemporary designs, and abstract shapes. Embellish a border with a vine and flowers, precisely place a bevy of butterflies, or replicate a vintage appliqué.

The choices you make will become your hallmark.

SCRAP
Apple

At the core of this creation is an abundant stash of scraps.

Designer Betty Lenz started the familiar Pineapple blocks with

a square of red fabric in each center. Then she allowed them

to grow with randomly selected leftovers. The appliquéd border

of blossoms echoes the red in the block centers.

Materials

³⁄₈ yard of solid dark red for block centers and
   flower appliqués .

7¹⁄₂ yards total of assorted medium and dark prints
   (minimum of 36 different prints) for blocks

2¹⁄₂ yards of assorted light prints (minimum
   of 12 different prints) for blocks

2⁵⁄₈ yards of tan print for borders and binding

2⁵⁄₈ yards of solid black for appliqué borders

⁵⁄₈ yard of dark stripe for vine appliqués

¹⁄₄ yard of brown print for vine tendril appliqués

Scraps of assorted prints in orange, brown, green, red,
   rose, peach, and burgundy for flower appliqués

¹⁄₈ yard of scraps of green-brown batik for leaf appliqués

Scraps of solid green for leaf appliqués

Scraps of crochet or lace for flower appliqués

Bronze and verdigris seed beads

6¹⁄₈ yards of backing fabric

87×98" of quilt batting

Tracing paper

Finished quilt top: 80¹⁄₂×91¹⁄₂"
Finished block: 5¹⁄₂" square

Quantities specified for 44/45"-wide, 100% cotton
fabrics. All measurements include a ¼" seam
allowance. Sew with right sides together unless
otherwise stated.

continued

Foundation-Piecing Method

Project designer Betty Lenz used foundation piecing to construct the Pineapple blocks in this quilt. To foundation-piece blocks, you stitch fabric pieces together on paper patterns, called foundation papers. When all the pieces for a block have been added, the foundation paper is torn away.

For this method you need a foundation paper for each block and fabric pieces that are at least ¼" larger on all sides than the areas they are to cover (indicated on the pattern by solid lines). Stitch with the right side of the foundation paper facing you and the fabric pieces underneath, right sides together. Use a tiny stitch length (12 to 16 stitches per inch). Then, when stitching is complete, the paper will easily tear away from the assembled block. You trim the fabric pieces to the correct size after stitching them to the foundation paper.

Make the Foundation Papers

Use tracing paper, a pencil, and a ruler to trace the Scrap Apple Quilt Foundation-Piecing Pattern, found on *Pattern Sheet 1*, 120 times. (We suggest tracing because photocopy machines may alter proportions.) Transfer all the pattern's lines and numbers to each foundation paper.

Cut the Fabrics

To make the best use of your fabrics, cut the pieces in the order that follows. Because foundation papers will stabilize the fabrics, don't worry about grain lines when cutting out fabric pieces.

From solid dark red, cut:
• 120—1¾" squares

From assorted medium and dark prints, cut:
• 240—1½×42" strips

From assorted light prints, cut:
• 60—1½×42" strips

Foundation-Piece the Blocks

1. For one Pineapple block you'll need a foundation paper, a solid dark red 1¾" square for the center, and 36 different light, medium, and dark print 1½×42" strips. Refer to the photograph of the quilt *opposite* for fabric placement ideas.

2. With wrong sides together, center the solid dark red 1¾" square over area No. 1 on the foundation paper. Remember, this and all subsequent pieces should cover the area within the solid lines plus

¼" beyond them. Hold the red square in place with your fingers, a pin, or a dab of glue from a glue stick.

3. Place a dark print 1½"-wide strip atop the red square with right sides together and raw edges aligned. With the paper right side up, stitch on the solid line between area No. 1 and an area No. 2, beginning and ending a few stitches beyond the ends of the line (see Photo 1).

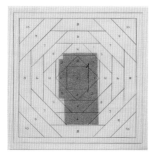

Photo I

Trim the seam allowance to a scant ¼". With the fabric side up, press the pieces open, pressing the seam allowance toward area No. 2 (see Photo 2). Trim the dark print piece to about ¼" beyond the solid lines around area No. 2.

Note: For photographic purposes, we used black thread to stitch these sample pieces. When you sew, we recommend you use thread in a color that matches your fabrics or a medium gray.

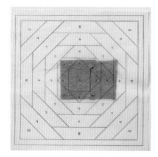

Photo 2

4. Position a second light, medium, or dark print 1½"-wide strip atop the first two pieces. Stitch on the line between area No. 1 and a second area No. 2. Trim and press as previously instructed. Add the third and fourth print strips, working in a clockwise direction and trimming and pressing as before (see Photo 3).

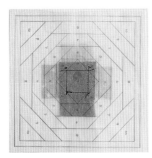

Photo 3

5. Continue adding the pieces to the foundation paper in the numerical order marked on the pattern (see photos 4, 5, and 6). Work in clockwise fashion; trim and press the seams after adding each strip to make a Pineapple block (see Photo 7). The pieced block should measure 6" square, including the seam allowances. Using the blunt edge of a seam ripper, carefully tear away the foundation paper.

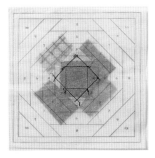

Photo 4   **Photo 5**

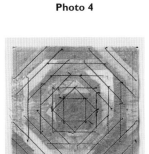

Photo 6   **Photo 7**

6. Repeat steps 1 through 5 to make a total of 120 Pineapple blocks.

Assemble the Quilt Center

Referring to the photograph *above* for placement, lay out the blocks in 12 rows. Sew together the blocks in each row. Press the seam allowances in one direction, alternating the direction with each

row. Then join the rows to make the quilt center. Press the seam allowances in one direction. The pieced quilt center should measure 55½×66½", including the seam allowances.

Add the Borders

Cut the border strips the length of the fabric (parallel to the selvage). The border measurements that follow are mathematically correct. Before cutting your border strips, measure your quilt top and adjust the lengths accordingly.

From tan print, cut:
- 2—1¾×55½" inner border strips
- 2—1¾×69" inner border strips
- 2—2½×77" outer border strips
- 2—2½×92" outer border strips

From solid black, cut:
- 2—10×80" appliqué border strips
- 2—10×90" appliqué border strips

continued

1. Sew the short tan print inner border strips to the top and bottom edges of the pieced quilt center. Press the seam allowances toward the tan print border. Then sew the long tan print inner border strips to the side edges of the pieced quilt center. Press the seam allowances toward the tan print border. The pieced quilt center should now measure 58×69", including the seam allowances.

2. With right sides together and midpoints aligned, pin a solid black 10×80" appliqué border strip to the top and bottom edges of the pieced quilt center and a solid black 10×90" appliqué border strip to each side edge; allow excess border fabric to extend beyond the edges. Sew each border strip to the quilt center, beginning and ending the seams ¼" from the corners. Press the seam allowances toward the black border strips.

3. Miter the black border's corners. For information on mitering, see the Mitered Border Corner instructions in Quilter's Schoolhouse, which begins on *page 150*.

4. Sew the short tan print outer border strips to the top and bottom edges of the quilt center. Press the seam allowances toward the tan print outer borders. Then sew the long tan print outer border strips to the side edges of the quilt center to complete the quilt top. Press the seam allowances toward the tan print outer border.

Appliqué the Border

Make templates of the appliqué patterns found on *Pattern Sheet 1* according to the instructions in Quilter's Schoolhouse, which begins on *page 150*.

From dark stripe, cut:
* 1—22×42" rectangle, cutting it into ⅞"-wide bias strips; piece the strips into one 340"-long strip for vine appliqués (For specific instructions on Cutting Bias Strips, see Quilter's Schoolhouse.)

From brown print, cut:
* 1—9×42" rectangle, cutting it into ¾"-wide bias strips for vine tendril appliqués

From solid dark red, cut:
* 10 of Pattern A
* 6 of Pattern M

Scrap Apple Quilt
optional sizes

If you'd like to make this quilt in a size other than for a double bed, use the information *below*. The border sizes for the wall hanging optional size do not allow for appliquéing in the border.

Alternate quilt sizes	Wall	Twin	King
Number of blocks	25	70	196
Number of blocks wide by long	5×5	7×10	14×14
Finished border width	1¾", 3", 2"	1¼", 9½", 2"	1¼", 9½", 2"
Finished size	40" square	64×80½"	102½" square
Yardage requirements			
Solid dark red	⅛ yard	⅓ yard	⅝ yard
Assorted medium and dark prints	1½ yards	4½ yards	12 yards
Assorted light prints	½ yard	1½ yards	4 yards
Assorted fabrics for appliqué	½ yard	1 yard	1 yard
Tan print for borders	1¼ yards	2⅜ yards	3⅛ yards
Solid black for appliqué borders	1⅛ yards	2⅔ yards	3¼ yards
Binding	⅓ yard	⅝ yard	⅞ yard
Backing	1⅓ yards	4⅞ yards	9⅛ yards
Batting	46" square	70×87"	109" square

From assorted orange prints, cut:
- 10 of Pattern B
- 30 of Pattern D

From assorted brown prints, cut:
- 10 of Pattern C

From assorted green prints, cut:
- 8 *each* of patterns F, F reversed, G, G reversed, K, L, and L reversed
- 10 of Pattern K reversed
- 4 of Pattern H

From red print, cut:
- 4 of Pattern I
- 6 of Pattern N

From rose print, cut:
- 24 of Pattern P

From peach print, cut:
- 24 of Pattern P

From burgundy print, cut:
- 8 of Pattern O

From green-brown batik, cut:
- 8 of Pattern E

From solid green, cut:
- 8 of Pattern Q

From crochet or lace, cut:
- 10 of Pattern B
- 4 of Pattern J
- 6 of Pattern N

1. Prepare each of the appliqué pieces and bias strips by pressing under a 3/16" seam allowance.

2. Referring to the Scrap Apple Appliqué Placement Diagram on *Pattern Sheet 1* for placement and the photograph on *page 125,* baste vines and flower pieces onto the solid black border. Begin with the bottom layers and work up.

3. Using small slip stitches and threads that match the fabrics, appliqué the vine and flower pieces in place. Gently press from the back.

Complete the Quilt
From remaining tan print, cut:
- 9—2½×42" binding strips

1. Layer the quilt top, batting, and backing according to the instructions in Quilter's Schoolhouse, which begins on *page 150.* Quilt as desired. Sew bronze seed beads on flowers and verdigris seed beads on leaves as indicated on the appliqué patterns.

2. Use the tan print 2½×42" strips to bind the quilt according to the instructions in Quilter's Schoolhouse.

optional colors

The appliqué takes center stage in this pastel creation. Then the Pineapple block border, made from high-contrast fabrics, draws out the more angular aspects of the block.

WEDDING QUILT

The gentle contrast between beige and cream

prints allows a circular pattern to emerge

from the Pineapple blocks.

Materials

¹/₈ yard of beige print No. 1 for block centers

2¹/₂ yards total of assorted cream and beige

    prints for blocks and pieced border

¹/₂ yard of solid cream for inner border

¹/₃ yard of beige print No. 2 for binding

1¹/₈ yards of backing fabric

38" square of quilt batting

Tracing paper

Gold perle cotton

4 yards of ¹/₈"-wide gold-and-white braid

Finished quilt top: 32" square

Cut the Fabrics

To make the best use of your fabrics, cut the pieces in the order that follows. Refer to Make the Foundation Papers on *page 124* to make a total of 16 foundation papers.

From beige print No. 1, cut:
- 16—1¾" squares

From assorted cream and beige prints, cut:
- 48—1½×42" strips
- 120—1½×2½" rectangles

From solid cream, cut:
- 2—3½×28½" inner border strips
- 2—3½×22½" inner border strips

From beige print No. 2, cut:
- 4—2½×42" binding strips

Assemble the Blocks

Referring to Foundation-Piecing Method and Foundation-Piece the Blocks on *page 124,* use the beige print 1¾" squares and the assorted cream and beige print 1½×42" strips to make a total of 16 Pineapple blocks.

Assemble the Quilt Center

Sew together the blocks in four rows. Press the seam allowances in one direction, alternating the direction with each row. Then join the rows to make the quilt center. Press the seam allowances in one direction. The pieced quilt center should measure 22½" square, including the seam allowances.

Add the Borders

1. Sew the solid cream 3½×22½" inner border strips to opposite edges of the pieced quilt center. Then join the solid cream 3½×28½" inner border strips to the remaining edges of the quilt center. Press all seam allowances toward the inner border.

2. Join the assorted cream and beige print 1½×2½" rectangles along long edges to make the following:
- 2—2½×43½" outer border strips
- 2—2½×28½" outer border strips

3. Sew the short outer border strips to opposite edges of the pieced quilt center. Then join the long outer border strips to the remaining edges of the quilt center to complete the quilt top. Press all seam allowances toward the inner border.

4. Referring to the photograph *above* for placement, machine-couch the gold-and-white braid and gold perle cotton on the inner border, interweaving the strands.

To machine-couch, position the decorative thread on the quilt top. Set your machine for zigzag stitch that is slightly wider than the thread being couched. Adjust the upper tension, if necessary, or run the bobbin thread through the finger on the bobbin to increase its tension. This will pull the needle thread to the quilt back, preventing the bobbin thread from showing on the quilt top. Zigzag-stitch over the decorative thread, making sure the swing of the needle pivots to either side of the couched thread as you stitch.

Complete the Quilt

1. Layer the quilt top, batting, and backing according to the instructions in Quilter's Schoolhouse, which begins on *page 150.* Quilt as desired.

2. Use the beige print 2½×42" strips to bind the quilt according to the instructions in Quilter's Schoolhouse.

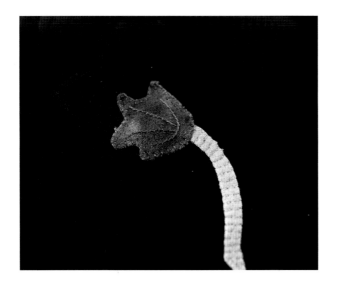

APPLIQUÉD COAT

Appliqué blossoms can bring a feeling of warmth to the coldest of days. Re-create the blooms in your favorite colors to add personality to a vest, skirt, or cape.

Materials

8" square of felted mauve wool for appliqués

5" square of felted bright pink wool for appliqués

4" square of felted soft pink wool for appliqués

3" square of felted cream wool for appliqués

7" square of felted olive green wool for appliqués

1/4 yard of felted teal blue wool for appliqués

8" square of felted light blue wool for appliqués

Purchased black wool coat

Embroidery floss to match appliqués

6 small mauve beads

Tracing paper

About the Wool

Felted wool is a favorite of quilters because its edges won't ravel when cut. The wools used in the photographed project were hand-dyed for a mottled appearance.

To felt your own wool, machine-wash it in a hot-water wash, cool-rinse cycle with a small amount of detergent; machine-dry and steam-press.

Cut the Fabrics

To make the best use of your fabrics, cut the pieces in the order that follows. This project uses "Scrap Apple" patterns, which are on *Pattern Sheet 1*. To make templates of the patterns, follow the instructions in Quilter's Schoolhouse, which begins on *page 150*. Do not add seam allowances when cutting out appliqué shapes from felted wool.

From mauve wool, cut:
- 2 of Pattern M
- 3 of Pattern D
- 1 of Pattern O

From bright pink wool, cut:
- 1 *each* of patterns A and O

From soft pink wool, cut:
- 2 of Pattern N

From cream wool, cut:
- 1 of Pattern B

From olive green wool, cut:
- 1 of Pattern E
- 2 of Pattern Q

From teal blue wool, cut:
- 1 *each* of patterns F and Q
- 1—9×42" rectangle, cutting it into enough 3/8"-wide bias strips to make the following (for specific instructions, see Cutting Bias Strips in Quilter's Schoolhouse):
  - 1 *each* of 17"-long, 10"-long, 9"-long, 7"-long, and 5"-long vines
  - 2—3"-long vines

From light blue wool, cut:
- 1 *each* of patterns C, F reversed, G reversed, K, and L
- 1—3/8×5" bias strip for vine

Appliqué the Coat

1. Referring to the photographs *above* and *opposite* for placement, baste vine, flower, and leaf pieces onto the coat front lapel and back. Begin with the bottom layer and work up.

2. Using two strands of matching embroidery floss, blanket-stitch around the flowers, leaves, and vines, being careful not to stitch through to the coat's lining.

To blanket-stitch, first pull your needle up at A, form a reverse L shape with the floss, and hold the angle of the L shape in place with your thumb. Then push your needle down at B and come up at C to secure the stitch.

Blanket Stitch

3. Sew mauve beads above the mauve flowers as shown in the photograph.

4. Using two strands of matching floss, stem-stitch the veins in the leaves to complete the coat.

To stem-stitch, pull your needle up at A. Insert your needle back into the fabric at B, about ⅜" away from A. Holding the thread out of the way, bring your needle back up at C and pull the thread through so it lies flat against the fabric. The distances between points A, B, and C should be equal. Pull with equal tautness after each stitch.

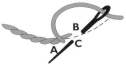

Stem Stitch

ANTIQUE *Peony*

American appliqué quilts crafted

between 1850 and 1880 often feature

vines and flowers, birds, and fruits.

This quilt, done in the bright red and

green fabrics that were in vogue then,

is an excellent example of work from

that era. The intricate appliqué,

backed by exquisite quilting,

demonstrates the quiltmaker's skill.

Materials

5½ yards of solid cream for appliqué foundations,
    setting triangles, and sashing
3¾ yards of solid dark green for appliqués, sashing,
    and border
2½ yards of solid red for appliqués, sashing,
    and border
5⅜ yards of backing fabric
85×98" of quilt batting

Finished quilt: 78¾×91⅛"
Finished block: 14½" square

Quantities specified for 44/45"-wide, 100% cotton fabrics. All measurements include a ¼" seam allowance. Sew with right sides together unless otherwise stated.

Quilt History

Either Abigail Bentley Larkin (1811–1898) or her daughter, Sarah Ann Larkin Marshall (1838–1908), both of Tolland, Massachusetts, could have made "Antique Peony," today part of the permanent collection of the New England Quilt Museum in Lowell, Massachusetts. Though it doesn't indicate what she was working on, Sarah's diary entry of March 8, 1870, reads: "At home all day quilting."

continued

"It's interesting to note the detail with which it was executed," museum curator Jennifer Gilbert says of the quilt. In all the squares, the stems are directed away from the quilt's center so that the flower groupings would remain upright when the quilt was draped over a bed—a reminder that quilts were once thought of only as bed coverings. The remarkable condition of the quilt indicates it was not used daily.

Cut the Fabrics

To make the best use of your fabrics, cut the pieces in the order that follows. The patterns are on *Pattern Sheet 2*. To make templates of the patterns, follow the instructions in Quilter's Schoolhouse, which begins on *page 150*. To use needle-turn appliqué, as was done in this project, add a ³⁄₁₆" seam allowance to all edges when cutting out the appliqué pieces.

The appliqué foundations are cut larger than necessary. You'll trim them to the correct size after completing the appliqué.

Cut the border strips the length of the fabric (parallel to the selvage). The border strip measurements are mathematically correct. You may wish to cut your strips longer than specified to allow for possible sewing differences.

From solid cream, cut:
- 3—21¾" squares, cutting each diagonally twice in an X to make a total of 12 large setting triangles (you'll have 1 leftover triangle)
- 15—16" squares for appliqué foundations
- 1—11⅛" square, cutting it in half diagonally to make a total of 2 small setting triangles
- 28—3½" squares for sashing

From solid dark green, cut:
- 2—2×87⅛" border strips
- 2—2×79¾" border strips
- 1—18×42" rectangle, cutting it into enough ⅝"-wide bias strips to total 850" in length (For specific instructions on cutting bias strips, see Quilter's Schoolhouse on *page 150*.)
- 84—1½×15" sashing strips
- 13—3¼" squares
- 246 of Pattern A
- 164 of Pattern B
- 26 *each* of patterns C, D, and D reversed
- 58 *each* of patterns F and H
- 13 *each* of patterns J and J reversed
- 56 of Pattern K

From solid red, cut:
- 2—1½×87⅛" border strips
- 2—1½×79¾" border strips
- 42—1½×15" strips for sashing
- 58 each of patterns E and G
- 13 each of patterns I and I reversed

Appliqué the Three-Peony Blocks

1. To appliqué one block you'll need one cream 16" square appliqué foundation, 14 green A leaves, four green B leaves, two green C leaves, two green D leaves, two green D reversed leaves, one green ⅝×13" bias strip, two green ⅝×3" bias strips, two green ⅝×6" bias strips, two green ⅝×4½" bias strips, three green F peony bases, two green H peony bud bases, one green 3¼" square, three red E peonies, and two red G peony buds.

2. Fold the cream 16" square foundation in half diagonally in both directions. Lightly finger-crease to create appliqué positioning guides; unfold.

3. Prepare the appliqué pieces, including the bias strips for stems, by basting under the ³⁄₁₆" seam allowances. Do not baste under seam allowances that will be covered by other pieces.

4. Baste the stem strips onto the foundation (see Diagram 1 for placement), using the creased lines as guides. Then pin the flower, flower base, and leaf pieces in place. To reduce bulk, trim the stems so that just ¼" runs under each flower.

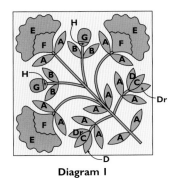

Diagram 1

5. Using small slip stitches and threads that match the fabrics, appliqué the pieces in place, starting with the stems and working from the bottom layer to the top layer.

6. Trim the appliquéd foundation to 15" square, including the seam allowances.

7. Fold the green 3¼" square in half diagonally. Lightly finger-crease to create a stitching guide; unfold. Align the green 3¼" square in the corner of the appliquéd square where the main stem ends (see Diagram 2, noting placement of the diagonal crease). Stitch on the crease; trim the seam allowance to ¼". Press the attached triangle open to complete an appliquéd three-peony block.

Diagram 2

8. Repeat steps 1 through 7 to make a total of 13 appliquéd three-peony blocks.

Appliqué the Four-Peony Blocks

1. To appliqué one four-peony block you'll need one cream 16" square appliqué foundation, eight green A leaves, eight green B leaves, four green F peony bases, four green H peony bud bases, two green ⁵⁄₈×9½" bias strips, two green ⁵⁄₈×8¼" bias strips, four red E peonies, and four red G peony buds.

2. Fold the cream 16" square foundation in half diagonally in both directions; lightly finger-crease and unfold.

3. Prepare the appliqué pieces, including the bias strips for stems, as before.

4. Baste the stem strips onto the foundation (see Diagram 3 for placement).

Diagram 3

5. Appliqué the pieces in place, starting with the stems.

6. Trim the appliqué foundation to 15" square, including the seam allowances, to complete an appliquéd four-peony block.

7. Repeat steps 1 through 6 to make a second appliquéd four-peony block.

Appliqué the Large Setting Triangles

1. To appliqué one large setting triangle you'll need one cream large setting triangle for the appliqué foundation, four green A leaves, eight green B leaves, one green F peony base, two green H

continued

peony bud bases, one green J half peony base, one green J reversed half peony base, three ⅝×4½" green bias strips, one red E peony, one red I half peony, one red I reversed half peony, and two red G peony buds.

2. Fold the cream triangle foundation in half; finger-crease and unfold.

3. Prepare the appliqué pieces, including the bias strips for stems, as before.

4. Baste the stem strips onto the foundation (see Diagram 4 for placement).

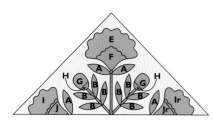

Diagram 4

5. Appliqué the pieces in place, starting with the stems, to complete an appliquéd large setting triangle.

6. Repeat steps 1 through 5 to make a total of 11 appliquéd large setting triangles.

Appliqué the Small Setting Triangles

1. To appliqué one small setting triangle you'll need one cream small setting triangle for the appliqué foundation, two green A leaves, four green B leaves, one green ⅝×5¼" bias strip, one green H peony bud base, one green J half peony base, one green J reversed half peony base, one red G peony bud, one red I half peony, and one red I reversed half peony.

2. Fold the cream triangle foundation in half; finger-crease and unfold.

3. Prepare appliqué pieces, including the bias strip for a stem, as before.

4. Baste the stem strip onto the foundation (see Diagram 5 for placement).

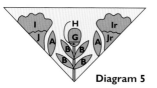

Diagram 5

5. Appliqué the pieces in place, starting with the stem, to complete an appliquéd small setting triangle.

6. Repeat steps 1 through 5 to make a second appliquéd small setting triangle.

Appliqué the Sashing Squares

1. For one sashing square you'll need one cream 3½" square and two green K leaves.

2. Fold the cream 3½" square in half diagonally in both directions; finger-crease and unfold.

3. Prepare appliqué pieces as before.

4. Appliqué the bottom leaf in place (see Diagram 6). Appliqué the second leaf at a 90° angle to the first leaf to complete an appliquéd sashing square.
   Note: It is not necessary to cut away the overlapped area of the bottom leaf.

Diagram 6

5. Repeat steps 1 through 4 to make a total of 28 appliquéd sashing squares.

Piece the Sashing Units

1. Aligning long edges, sew a green 1½×15" strip to each long edge of a red 1½×15" strip to make a sashing unit. Press the seam allowances toward the green strips. The pieced sashing unit should measure 3½×15", including seam allowances.

2. Repeat Step 1 to make a total of 42 sashing units.

Assemble the Quilt Center

1. Referring to the Quilt Assembly Diagram for placement, lay out the 13 three-peony blocks, the two four-peony blocks, the 11 large setting triangles, the two small setting triangles, the 28 sashing squares, and the 42 sashing units in diagonal rows.

2. Sew together the pieces in each diagonal row. Press the seam allowances toward the sashing units. Then join the rows to make the quilt center. Press the seam allowances in one direction.

3. Trim the edges, leaving a ¼" seam allowance beyond the pieced block corners. The pieced quilt center should measure 74¾×87⅛", including the seam allowances.

Add the Border

1. Join one green 2×87⅛" border strip and one red 1½×87⅛" border strip to make a side border unit. Press the seam allowance toward the green strip. Repeat to make a second side border unit.

2. Join one green 2×79¾" border strip and one red 1½×79¾" border strip to make a top border unit. Repeat to make a bottom border unit. Press the seam allowances toward the green strips.

3. Sew the side border units to the side edges of the pieced quilt center (the red strip should be on the inside). Then add the top and bottom border units to the top and bottom edges of the pieced quilt center to complete the quilt top (the red strip should be on the inside). Press all seam allowances toward the pieced border.

Complete the Quilt

1. Layer the quilt top, batting, and backing according to the instructions in Quilter's Schoolhouse, which begins on *page 150*.

2. Quilt as desired to within ¾" of the quilt's outer edges. To finish, trim batting and backing ¾" smaller on all edges than the quilt top. Turn the border under ⅜" twice and slip-stitch to the backing.

Quilt Assembly Diagram

Antique Peony Quilt
optional sizes

If you'd like to make this quilt in a size other than for a double bed, use the information *below*.

Alternate quilt sizes	Wall	King
Number of blocks	5	25
Number of blocks wide by long	2×2 with 1 center	4×4 with 3 centers
Finished size	54" square	103½" square
Yardage requirements		
Solid cream	2⅜ yards	7¾ yards
Solid dark green	2½ yards	4½ yards
Solid red	1⅞ yards	3¼ yards
Backing	3⅓ yards	9¼ yards
Batting	60" square	110" square

PEONY WALL HANGING

Appliquéd flowers burst from a sunshine-yellow background in this contemporary wall hanging. The vine and flowers on the sky-blue inner border mimic the curves of the scalloped outer border.

Materials

I yard total of assorted blue prints for appliqués and inner border corner squares

18×22" (fat quarter) of pink print for appliqués

9×22" (fat eighth) of dark pink print for appliqués

18×22" (fat quarter) of orange tone-on-tone print for appliqués

9×22" (fat eighth) of orange stripe for appliqués

⅛ yard total of assorted yellow prints for appliqués

¼ yard *each* of two light green prints for appliqué foundations and sashing

¼ yard of bright yellow print for sashing

¼ yard of orange print for inner border

½ yard of light blue print for middle border

1½ yards of large floral for outer border

½ yard of lime green print for binding

3 yards of backing fabric

57×53" of quilt batting

I yard of lightweight fusible web

Finished size: 51×46½"

Cut the Fabrics

To make the best use of your fabrics, cut the pieces in the order that follows.

This project uses "Antique Peony" patterns on *Pattern Sheet 2*. To make templates of these patterns, follow the instructions in Quilter's Schoolhouse, which begins on *page 150*.

To use fusible web for appliquéing, as was done in this project, complete the following steps.

1. Lay the fusible web, paper side up, over the patterns. With a pencil, trace each pattern the number of times indicated *opposite*, leaving ½" between tracings. Cut out the pieces roughly ¼" outside of the traced lines.

2. Following the manufacturer's instructions, press the fusible-web pieces onto the backs of the

designated fabrics; let cool. Cut out the fabric pieces on the drawn lines. Peel off the paper backings.

From assorted blue prints, cut:
- 1—10" square, cutting it into enough ¾"-wide bias strips to make six ¾×7" strips for large flower stems (For specific instructions on cutting bias strips, see Quilter's Schoolhouse.)
- 1—14" square, cutting it into enough ¾"-wide bias strips to make a 200"-long vine appliqué
- 20 of Pattern A
- 35 of Pattern B
- 16 of Pattern H
- 4—2" squares

From pink print, cut:
- 3 of Pattern E

From dark pink print, cut:
- 3 of Pattern F

From orange tone-on-tone print, cut:
- 3 of Pattern E

From orange stripe, cut:
- 3 of Pattern F

From assorted yellow prints, cut:
- 16 of Pattern G

From *each* light green print, cut:
- 3—8½×10½" rectangles for appliqué foundations
- 2—1" squares

From bright yellow print, cut:
- 2—1×25½" sashing strips
- 4—1×21" sashing strips
- 3—1×8½" sashing strips

From orange print, cut:
- 2—2×26½" inner border strips
- 2—2×22" inner border strips

From light blue print, cut:
- 2—4½×37½" middle border strips
- 2—4½×25" middle border strips

From large floral, cut:
- 2—7½×51½" outer border strips
- 2—7½×33" outer border strips

From lime green print, cut:
- 1—18×24" rectangle, cutting it into enough 2½"-wide bias strips to total 210" in length

Appliqué the Blocks

1. Prepare the blue print stem and vine appliqué pieces by basting under a ³⁄₁₆" seam allowance. Set aside the vine appliqué piece.

2. Referring to the Appliqué Placement Diagram, arrange a prepared stem on a light green 8½×10½" rectangle; baste. Machine-blanket-stitch the stem in place. Arrange the remaining appliqué pieces on the foundation; fuse. Machine-blanket-stitch the remaining appliqué pieces in place to complete an appliquéd block.

Appliqué Placement Diagram

3. Repeat Step 2 to make a total of six appliquéd blocks.

Assemble the Quilt Center

1. Referring to the photograph *opposite*, lay out the six appliquéd blocks and three bright yellow print 1×8½" sashing strips in vertical rows. Join the rows with two bright yellow print 1×21" sashing strips between the rows to make a pieced block unit. Press all seam allowances toward the sashing strips.

2. Add the bright yellow print 1×25½" sashing strips to the top and bottom edges of the pieced block unit. Join a light green print 1" square to each end of the remaining bright yellow print 1×21" sashing strips to make two sashing units. Add the sashing units to the side edges of the pieced block unit to complete the quilt center.

Add the Borders

1. Sew the orange print 2×26½" inner border strips to the top and bottom edges of the quilt center. Join a blue print 2" square to each end of the orange print 2×22" inner border strips to make inner border units. Add the inner border units to the side edges of the quilt center.

2. Sew the light blue print 4½×25" middle border strips to the side edges of the quilt center. Then add the light blue print 4½×37½" middle border strips to the top and bottom edges of the quilt center. Press all seam allowances toward the middle border.

3. Sew the large floral 7½×33" outer border strips to the side edges of the quilt center. Then add the large floral 7½×51½" outer border strips to the top and bottom edges of the quilt center. Press all seam allowances toward the middle border.

continued

Appliqué the Borders

1. Referring to the photograph on *page 138* for placement, lay the prepared vine appliqué on the light blue middle border; baste. Machine-blanket-stitch in place.

2. Arrange the remaining appliqué pieces along the vine; fuse. Machine-blanket-stitch in place.

Complete the Quilt

Mark the scallops on the large floral outer border according to the following instructions. Do not cut the scallops until after quilting is completed.

1. Draw the desired scallop on a strip of paper as long as a border. Place three dots approximately 17" apart on the top edge of the paper to mark the top of each scallop. Draw a line between these dots. Make another set of dots 3½" directly below the first marks. The depth between the first and second marks is the depth of the scallops.

2. Using a compass, jar lid, plate, or other rounded edge as a guide, join the second set of marks with a gentle curve that just touches the line drawn between the first set of marks.

3. Once you've created a scallop you like, draw it along the complete length of the paper strip to make a border template. Repeat to make a side border template.

4. Position the paper templates on the quilt top outer border and check the corners. You'll need to blend the curves of the scallops to round the corners. Once you've blended the edges of one corner, make a paper template of it and trace three more identical paper templates for the remaining corners. Use your paper templates to mark the pattern on your quilt top outer border.

5. Hand- or machine-quilt as desired. Trim the outer border according to the marked scallops, leaving ¼" beyond the drawn line.

6. Use the lime green print 2½"-wide bias strips to bind the quilt according to the instructions in Quilter's Schoolhouse, which begins on *page 150.*

CURTAINS

Stars will shine throughout the day with these homespun curtains of blue ticking edged in stripes.

Materials to Make Two Panels

⅛ yard of solid blue homespun for star appliqués

⅛ yard of solid tan homespun for appliqué foundations

¼ yard of red, tan, and blue stripe for curtain trim

1¾ yards of blue ticking for curtains and tabs

1½ yards of solid tan for backing

¼ yard of lightweight fusible web

Finished size: 24×36" each curtain panel

Cut the Fabrics

To make the best use of your fabrics, cut the pieces in the order that follows. *Note:* To make this project for an alternate window size, cut your curtain and trim fabrics the necessary length and width, then adjust the number of tabs as desired.

This project uses "Antique Peony" pattern K on *Pattern Sheet 2*. To make a template of this pattern, follow the instructions in Quilter's Schoolhouse, which begins on *page 150*.

To use fusible web for appliquéing, as was done in this project, complete the following steps.

1. Lay the fusible web, paper side up, over Pattern K. With a pencil, trace the pattern 16 times, leaving ½" between tracings. Cut out the pieces roughly ¼" outside of the traced lines.

2. Following the manufacturer's instructions, press the fusible-web pieces onto the back of the solid blue homespun; let cool. Cut out the fabric pieces on the drawn lines. Peel off the paper backings.

From solid tan homespun, cut:
• 8—3½" square appliqué foundations
From red, tan, and blue stripe, cut:
• 4—3½×18" trim strips
From blue ticking, cut:
• 2—24½×30½" rectangles
• 10—3¼×6" rectangles
From solid tan, cut:
• 2—24½×36½" rectangles

Appliqué the Corner Squares

1. Fold the solid tan homespun 3½" squares in half diagonally in both directions; finger-crease and unfold.

2. Referring to Diagram 6 on *page 136*, fuse a prepared solid blue K leaf to a solid tan 3½" square following the manufacturer's instructions. Fuse a second solid blue K leaf at a 90° angle to the first leaf. Let the fabrics cool. Using matching thread, machine-satin-stitch the appliqué edges to complete a corner square. Repeat to make a total of eight corner squares.

Complete the Curtain

1. Sew an appliquéd 3½" corner square to each end of the red, tan, and blue stripe 3½×18" trim strips. Sew the trim strips to the top and bottom edges of the blue ticking 24½×30½" rectangles to make two curtain panels.

2. Fold a blue ticking 3¼×6" rectangle in half lengthwise with the right sides inside; sew together the long raw edges. Turn right side

out. Move the seam to the center back and press to make a hanging tab. Fold the tab in half crosswise. Repeat to make a total of 10 hanging tabs.

3. Position the hanging tabs along the top edge of each curtain panel; align raw edges and baste in place.

4. With right sides together, layer each curtain panel with a solid tan 24½×36½" rectangle. The hanging tabs should be sandwiched between the two layers. Sew together, leaving a 6" opening in one side for turning, to make two lined curtain panels. Turn the curtain panels right side out; press. Slip stitch the opening closed.

This bevy of butterflies framed by a garden of tulips

will keep spring in the air year-round. The overlay method

of appliqué, perfected by the design team of Becky Goldsmith

and Linda Jenkins, assures the accurate placement

of each butterfly and flower.

BUTTERFLY *Garden*

Materials

1⅞ yards of muslin for appliqué foundations
and inner border

Scraps of assorted purple, yellow, green, pink,
red, blue, orange, and tan for appliqués

⅓ yard of green pin dot for appliqués and
inner border

⅓ yard of green stripe for appliqués

⅓ yard of green polka dot for binding

41" square of backing fabric

41" square of quilt batting

Embroidery floss in colors to match the appliqués

¼ yard of clear upholstery vinyl or other
clear flexible plastic (optional)

Finished quilt top: 35" square
Finished block: 5" square

Quantities specified for 44/45"-wide, 100% cotton
fabrics. All measurements include a ¼" seam
allowance. Sew with right sides together unless
otherwise indicated.

continued

Designer Notes

Over the years, project designers Becky Goldsmith and Linda Jenkins have developed their own appliqué method, which uses an overlay for placement purposes. The following instructions are for their overlay method. Your favorite appliqué method also can be used.

They advise pairing fabrics before cutting to make sure you have enough coordinating prints.

Make the Appliqué Templates

1. The patterns are on *Pattern Sheet 1*. Accurately trace pattern pieces 1 through 14 onto template plastic.

2. Cut out the templates on the drawn lines with sharp scissors. Becky and Linda stress the importance of keeping template edges smooth and points sharp.

3. Mark the right side of each template with the proper number. The numbers indicate the appliquéing sequence.

Cut the Fabrics

To make the best use of your fabrics, cut the pieces in the order that follows.

The appliqué foundations are cut larger than necessary to allow for sewing differences. You'll trim the foundations to the correct size after completing the appliqué.

When cutting out the appliqué pieces, lay the fabrics and template with right sides up; trace. Add a ³⁄₁₆" seam allowance to all edges when cutting out the appliqué pieces.

Cut the border strips the length of the fabric (parallel to the selvage). The border strip measurements are mathematically correct. You may wish to cut your border strips longer than specified to allow for possible sewing differences.

From muslin, cut:
- 4—7×27" rectangles for border appliqué foundations
- 4—1¾×40" strips for inner border
- 20—7" squares for appliqué foundations

From assorted purple, yellow, and green print scraps, cut:
- 6 *each* of patterns 1, 2, 3, and 4

From assorted pink and red print scraps, cut:
- 20 of Pattern 14
- 6 *each* of patterns 1, 2, 3, and 4

From assorted blue print scraps, cut:
- 28 of Pattern 7
- 3 *each* of patterns 1, 2, 3, and 4

From assorted orange print scraps, cut:
- 1 *each* of patterns 1, 2, 3, and 4
- 4 of Pattern 8

From assorted tan print scraps, cut:
- 16 of Pattern 5

From green pin dot, cut:
- 4—1¾×40" strips for inner border
- 4 of Pattern 6
- 20 of Pattern 11

From green stripe, cut:
- 20 *each* of patterns 12 and 13
- 4 *each* of patterns 9 and 10

From green polka dot, cut:
- 4—2½×40" binding strips

From upholstery vinyl, cut:
- 3—5" squares

Appliqué the Blocks and Outer Border

1. Lightly press the muslin 7" squares in half horizontally and vertically to form placement lines; unfold.

2. Position a vinyl 5" square over the Butterfly Appliqué Placement Diagram on *Pattern Sheet 1*, and accurately trace the design once, including the dashed placement lines, with a permanent marker.

3. Position the overlay on a creased muslin 7" foundation square, orienting the overlay's placement lines with the pressed lines. Pin the top of the overlay to the fabric, if desired.

4. Slide a Pattern 1 wing piece, right side up, between the foundation square and the overlay. Be sure to leave enough fabric at one end so pattern pieces 3 and 5 can cover it. When the wing piece is in place, remove the overlay, pin the wing to the foundation, and appliqué it in place.

5. Use the overlay to position the next piece in the stitching sequence. Working in numerical order, continue in this manner—positioning the pieces right side up under the overlay, removing the overlay to pin them to the background, and appliquéing them in place—until a butterfly block is completed.

6. Backstitch the butterfly antennae using one strand of floss and tiny stitches. Becky and Linda matched the floss color to the color of the butterfly's wings.

7. Press the appliquéd butterfly block from the back; trim it to measure 5½" square, including the seam allowances.

8. Repeat steps 3 through 7 to make a total of 16 appliquéd butterfly blocks.

9. Repeat steps 2 through 5, tracing the Daisy Appliqué Placement Diagram on *Pattern Sheet 1*, to make a total of four appliquéd daisy blocks. Press the appliquéd daisy blocks. Trim each one to measure 5½" square, including the seam allowances.

10. Lightly press a muslin 7×27" rectangle in half horizontally and vertically to form placement lines. Press two additional vertical placement lines on either side of the center crease, evenly spacing them 4¾" apart, to make a total of five vertical placement lines. Lightly press the same placement lines in the remaining three muslin 7×27" rectangles.

11. Referring to the photograph *above right* for placement, repeat steps 2 through 5, tracing the Tulip Appliqué Placement Diagram on *Pattern Sheet 1*, to appliqué five tulips on each creased muslin 7×27" foundation rectangle. Press the appliquéd tulip rectangles. Trim each to measure 5½×25½", including the seam allowances, to make a total of four appliquéd tulip border strips.

Assemble the Quilt Center

1. Referring to the photograph for placement, lay out the butterfly blocks in four horizontal rows. Sew together the blocks in each row. Press the seam allowances in one direction, alternating the direction with each row.

2. Join the rows to make the quilt center. Press the seam allowances in one direction. The pieced

quilt center should measure 20½" square, including the seam allowances.

Assemble and Add the Inner Border

1. Aligning long edges, sew together one green pin-dot 1¾×40" strip and one muslin 1¾×40" strip to make a strip set (see Diagram 1). Press the seam allowance toward the green pin dot strip. Repeat to make a total of four strip sets.

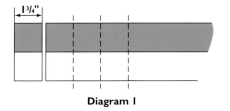

1¾"

Diagram 1

2. Cut the strip sets into a total of seventy-two 1¾"-wide segments.

continued

3. Join sixteen 1¾"-wide segments in a row to make a checkerboard border strip (see Diagram 2). The pieced checkerboard border strip should measure 3×20½", including the seam allowances. Repeat to make a second checkerboard border strip of the same size. Sew the checkerboard border strips to opposite edges of the pieced quilt center. Press the seam allowances toward the checkerboard border.

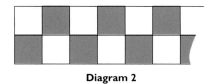

Diagram 2

4. Sew together twenty 1¾"-wide segments to make a checkerboard border strip that measures 3×25½", including the seam allowances. Repeat to make second checkerboard border strip of the same size. Sew these checkerboard border strips to the remaining edges of the pieced quilt center. Press the seam allowances toward the checkerboard border.

Add the Outer Border

1. Referring to the photograph on *page 145*, sew an appliquéd tulip border strip to opposite edges of the pieced quilt center. Press the seam allowances toward the appliquéd border.

2. Sew an appliquéd daisy block to each end of the remaining appliquéd tulip border strips to make two border units. Sew the border units to the remaining edges of the pieced quilt center to complete the quilt top. Press the seam allowances toward the appliquéd border.

Complete the Quilt

1. Layer the quilt top, batting, and backing according to the instructions in Quilter's Schoolhouse, which begins on *page 150*.

2. Quilt as desired. Becky and Linda echo-quilted the butterfly, tulip, and daisy appliqués. In addition, to add contrast to the many curves in the quilt, they quilted an X on each muslin square in the checkerboard border.

3. Use the green polka-dot 2½×40" strips to bind the quilt according to the instructions in Quilter's Schoolhouse.

Butterfly Garden Quilt
optional sizes

If you'd like to make this quilt in a size other than for a wall hanging, use the information *below*.

Alternate quilt sizes	Twin	Full/Queen	King
Number of blocks	126	224	324
Number of blocks wide by long	9×14	14×16	18×18
Finished size	60×85"	85×95"	105" square
Yardage requirements			
Muslin—borders cut the length of fabric	7½ yards	10½ yards	13⅞ yards
Assorted fabrics for appliqués	3 yards	5½ yards	9 yards
Green pin dot	¾ yard	⅞ yard	1 yard
Green stripe for appliqués	1 yard	2 yards	2⅞ yards
Binding	⅝ yard	⅔ yard	⅞ yard
Backing	5⅛ yards	7⅝ yards	9¼ yards
Batting	66×91"	91×101"	111" square

TULIP PILLOW

When textured fabrics are combined with the simple appliqué shapes,

the results are a graphic decorating accessory.

Materials

¹/₈ yard of gold print for tulip appliqués

¹/₈ yard of textured green solid for appliqué
   foundations

1¹/₂ yards of textured beige solid for pillow
   top and back

Gold embroidery floss

18×14" pillow form

Scraps of fusible web

Finished pillow: 23×19"

Cut the Fabrics

To make the best use of your fabrics, cut the pieces
in the order that follows.

To use fusible web for appliquéing, as was done
in this project, use the following steps.

1. Lay the fusible web, paper side up, over "Butterfly
Garden" patterns on *Pattern Sheet 1*. With a
pencil, trace the patterns as indicated *below*,
leaving ¹/₂" between tracings. Cut out the pieces
roughly ¹/₄" outside the traced lines.

2. Following the manufacturer's instructions, press
the fusible-web shapes onto the back of the gold
print; let cool. Cut out the pieces on the drawn
lines. Peel off the paper backings.

From gold print, cut:
* 3 of Pattern 14
* 3 *each* of patterns 12 and 13

From textured green solid, cut:
* 3—3×6" rectangles
* 2—¾×4" rectangles

continued

From textured beige solid, cut:
- 2—29×20" rectangles
- 1—24×20" rectangle

Appliqué the Pillow Top

1. Fringe the four sides of the green 3×6" rectangles. Center a fringed green rectangle atop the textured beige 24×20" rectangle. With three strands of gold embroidery floss, secure the green rectangle to the beige rectangle with a running stitch.

   To make a running stitch, pull your needle up at A (see diagram *below*) and insert it back into the fabric at B, ⅛" away from A. Pull your needle up at C, ⅛" from B, and repeat.

Running Stitch

2. Position the remaining fringed green rectangles 1" away from the stitched green rectangle; stitch in place in the same manner to make the pillow top.

3. Position the prepared appliqué pieces on the stitched pillow top; fuse in place.

4. With gold embroidery floss, backstitch each appliqué piece in place.

   To backstitch, pull the needle up at A. Insert it back into the fabric at B, and bring it up at C. Push the needle down again at D, and bring it up at E. Continue in the same manner.

Backstitch

5. With gold embroidery floss, chain-stitch a stem for each tulip.

   To chain-stitch, pull your needle up at A (see diagram *below*), form a U shape with the floss, and hold the shape in place with your thumb. Push your needle down at B, about ⅛" from A, and come up at C. Continue in the same manner.

Chain Stitch

6. Tie each textured green cotton ¾×4" rectangle in a knot. Referring to the photograph on *page 147*, secure the knotted rectangles to the pillow top.

7. With wrong sides inside, fold each textured beige 29×20" rectangle in half to form two double-thick 14½×20" pieces. Overlap the folded edges by 5". Stitch ½" from the top and bottom edges, including across the folds, to secure the pieces and create the pillow back.

8. Layer the pillow top and the pillow back. Sew the pieces together along all four edges using a ½" seam allowance to make the pillow cover; turn right side out. Press the pillow cover, making sure the corners are sharp.

9. Machine-stitch through the pillow cover layers at 5⁄16" intervals to make the flange. Stitch three rows using light green thread, then stitch a row using gold thread. Repeat this stitching sequence. The inside measurement of the last row of stitching should make a 18×14" rectangle.

10. Insert the pillow form through the back opening.

BUTTERFLY LINENS

Embellish a sheet set with butterflies

and flowers for an ensemble that will

brighten any room.

Materials

⅛ yard of green pin dot for appliqués

⅛ yard of green stripe for appliqués

Scraps of assorted yellow, pink, orange, red, teal,
   blue, and purple prints for appliqués

Embroidery floss to match the appliqués

Twin flat sheet

Two standard pillowcases

Machine embroidery thread in matching colors

1 yard of fusible web

Finished sheet: 64×100"
Finished pillowcase: 20×30"

These appliqués were made for a twin-size sheet
and standard pillowcases. Make more or fewer
appliqués depending upon the width of your sheet
and size of your pillowcases.

Cut the Fabrics

To make the best use of your fabrics, cut the pieces
in the order that follows.

   To use fusible web for appliquéing, as was done
in this project, use the following steps.

1. Lay the fusible web, paper side up, over "Butterfly
   Garden" patterns on *Pattern Sheet 1*. With a
   pencil, trace the patterns as indicated *below*,
   leaving ½" between tracings. Cut out the pieces
   roughly ¼" outside the traced lines.

2. Following the manufacturer's instructions, press
   the fusible-web shapes onto the back of the
   designated fabrics; let cool. Cut out the pieces on
   the drawn lines. Peel off the paper backings.

From green pin dot, cut:
- 4 *each* of patterns 12 and 13
- 8 of Pattern 11

From green stripe, cut:
- 4 *each* of patterns 9 and 10

From assorted yellow, pink, orange, red, teal, blue,
and purple print scraps, cut:
- 8 of Pattern 14
- 8 sets of 7 of Pattern 7
- 8 of Pattern 8
- 5 *each* of patterns 1, 2, 3, 4, and 5

Appliqué the Sheet and Pillowcases

1. Referring to the photographs *opposite* and *above*
   for placement, position the prepared appliqué
   pieces on the pillowcases and flat sheet; fuse in
   place.

2. Machine satin-stitch around each of the appliqué
   shapes to complete the sheet set. Use a smaller
   satin-stitch to create the butterfly antennae.

QUILTER'S SCHOOLHOUSE

GETTING STARTED

Before you begin any project, collect the tools and materials

you'll need in one place.

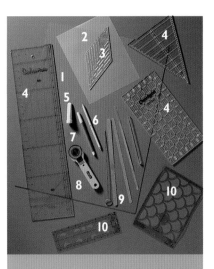

Basic Tools
1. Rotary-cutting mat
2. Template plastic
3. Template
4. Acrylic rulers
5. Chalk marker
6. Marking pencil
7. Water-erasable marker
8. Rotary cutter
9. Bias bars
10. Quilting stencils

Tools

CUTTING
Acrylic ruler: For making perfectly straight cuts with a rotary cutter, choose a ruler of thick, clear plastic. Many sizes are available. A 6×24" ruler marked in ¼" increments with 30°, 45°, and 60° angles is a good first purchase.

Rotary-cutting mat: A rotary cutter should always be used with a mat designed specifically for it. In addition to protecting the table, the mat helps keep the fabric from shifting while you cut. Often these mats are described as self-healing, meaning the blade does not leave slash marks or grooves in the surface, even after repeated usage. While many shapes and styles are available, a 16×23" mat marked with a 1" grid, with hash marks at ⅛" increments and 45° and 60° angles is a good choice.

Rotary cutter: The round blade of a rotary cutter will cut up to six layers of fabric at once. Because the blade is so sharp, be sure to purchase one with a safety guard and keep the guard over the blade when you're not cutting. The blade can be removed from the handle and replaced when it gets dull. Commonly available in three sizes, a good first blade is a 45mm.

Scissors: You'll need one pair for fabric and another for paper and plastic.

Pencils and other marking tools: Marks made with special quilt markers are easy to remove after sewing.

Template plastic: This slightly frosted plastic comes in sheets about ¹⁄₁₆" thick.

PIECING
Iron and ironing board

Sewing thread: Use 100-percent-cotton thread.

Sewing machine: Any machine in good working order with well-adjusted tension will produce pucker-free patchwork seams.

APPLIQUÉ
Fusible web: Instead of the traditional method, secure cutout shapes to the background of an appliqué block with this iron-on adhesive.

Hand-sewing needles: For hand appliqué, most quilters like fine quilting needles.

HAND QUILTING
Frame or hoop: You'll get smaller, more even stitches if you stretch your quilt as you stitch. A frame supports the quilt's weight, ensures even tension, and frees both your hands for stitching. However, once set up, it cannot be disassembled until the quilting is complete. Quilting hoops are more portable and less expensive.

Quilting needles: A "between" or quilting needle is short with a small eye. Common sizes are 8, 9, and 10; size 8 is best for beginners.

Quilting thread: Quilting thread is stronger than sewing thread.

Thimble: This finger cover relieves the pressure required to push a needle through several layers of fabric and batting.

MACHINE QUILTING

Darning foot: You may find this tool, also called a hopper foot, in your sewing machine's accessory kit. If not, have the model and brand of your machine available when you go to purchase one. It is used for free-motion stitching.

Safety pins: They hold the layers together during quilting.

Table: Use a large work surface that's level with your machine bed.

Thread: Use 100-percent-cotton quilting thread, cotton-wrapped polyester quilting thread, or very fine nylon monofilament thread.

Walking foot: This sewing-machine accessory helps you keep long, straight quilting lines smooth and pucker-free.

Choose Your Fabrics

It is no surprise that most quilters prefer 100-percent-cotton fabrics for quiltmaking. Cotton fabric minimizes seam distortion, presses crisply, and is easy to quilt. Most patterns, including those in this book, specify quantities for 44/45"-wide fabrics unless otherwise noted. Our projects call for a little extra yardage in length to allow for minor errors and slight shrinkage.

Prepare Your Fabrics

There are conflicting opinions about the need to prewash fabric. The debate is a modern one because most antique quilts were made with unwashed fabric. However, the dyes and sizing used today are unlike those used a century ago.

Prewashing fabric offers quilters certainty as its main advantage. Today's fabrics resist bleeding and shrinkage, but some of both can occur in some fabrics—an unpleasant prospect once you've assembled the quilt. Some quilters find prewashed fabric easier to quilt. If you choose to prewash your fabric, press it well before cutting.

Other quilters prefer the crispness of unwashed fabric for machine piecing. And, if you use fabrics with the same fiber content throughout the quilt, then any shrinkage that occurs in its first washing should be uniform. Some quilters find this small amount of shrinkage desirable, since it gives the quilt a slightly puckered, antique look.

We recommend you prewash a scrap of each fabric to test it for shrinkage and bleeding. If you choose to prewash a fabric, unfold it to a single layer. Wash it in warm water to allow the fabric to shrink and/or bleed. If the fabric bleeds, rinse it until the water runs clear. Don't use any fabric in your quilt if it hasn't stopped bleeding. Hang fabric to dry, or tumble it in the dryer until slightly damp.

Select the Batting

For a small beginner project, a thin cotton batting is a good choice. It has a tendency to "stick" to fabric so it requires less basting. Also, it's easy to stitch. It's wise to follow the stitch density (distance between rows of stitching required to keep the batting from shifting and wadding up inside the quilt) recommendation printed on the packaging.

Polyester batting is lightweight and readily available. In general, it springs back to its original height when compressed, adding a puffiness to quilts. It tends to "beard" (work out between the weave of the fabric) more than natural fibers. Polyester fleece is denser and works well for pillow tops and place mats.

Wool batting has good loft retention and absorbs moisture, making it ideal for cool, damp climates. Read the label carefully before purchasing a wool batting because it may require special handling.

ROTARY CUTTING

We've taken the guesswork out of rotary cutting with this primer.

Plan for Cutting

Quilt-Lovers' Favorites™ instructions list pieces in the order in which they should be cut to make the best use of your fabrics. Always consider the fabric grain before cutting. The arrow on a pattern piece or template indicates which direction the fabric grain should run. One or more straight sides of the pattern piece or template should follow the fabric's lengthwise or crosswise grain.

The lengthwise grain, parallel to the selvage (the tightly finished edge), has the least amount of stretch. (Do not use the selvage of a woven fabric in a quilt. When washed, it may shrink more than the rest of the fabric.) Crosswise grain, perpendicular to the selvage, has a little more give. The edge of any pattern piece that will be on the outside of a block or quilt should always be cut on the lengthwise grain. Be sure to press the fabric before cutting to remove any wrinkles or folds.

Using a Rotary Cutter

When cutting, keep an even pressure on the rotary cutter and make sure the blade is touching the edge of the ruler.

continued

The less you move your fabric when cutting, the more accurate you'll be.

SQUARING UP THE FABRIC EDGE

Before rotary-cutting fabric into strips, it is imperative that one fabric edge be made straight, or squared up. Since all subsequent cuts will be measured from this straight edge, squaring up the fabric edge is an important step. There are several different techniques for squaring up an edge, some of which involve the use of a pair of rulers. For clarity and simplicity, we have chosen to describe a single-ruler technique here. *Note:* The instructions as described are for right-handers.

1. Lay your fabric on the rotary mat with the right side down and one selvage edge away from you. Fold the fabric with the wrong side inside and the selvages together. Fold the fabric in half again, lining up the fold with the selvage edges. Lightly hand-crease all of the folds.

2. Position the folded fabric on the cutting mat with the selvage edges away from you and the bulk of the fabric length to your left. With the ruler on top of the fabric, align a horizontal grid line on the ruler with the lower folded fabric edge, leaving about 1" of fabric exposed along the right-hand edge of the ruler (see Photo 1). Do not worry about or try to align the uneven raw edges along the right-hand side of the fabric. *Note:* If the grid lines on the cutting mat interfere with your ability to focus on the ruler grid lines, turn your cutting mat over and work on the unmarked side.

3. Hold the ruler firmly in place with your left hand, keeping your fingers away from the right-hand edge and spreading your fingers apart slightly. Apply pressure to the ruler with your fingertips to prevent it from slipping as you cut. With the ruler firmly in place, hold the rotary cutter so the blade is touching the right-hand edge of the ruler. Roll the blade along the ruler edge, beginning just off the folded edge and pushing the cutter away from you, toward the selvage edge.

4. The fabric strip to the right of the ruler's edge should be cut cleanly away, leaving you with a straight edge from which you can measure all subsequent cuts. Do not pick up the fabric once the edge is squared; instead, turn the cutting mat to rotate the fabric and begin cutting strips.

CUTTING AND SUBCUTTING STRIPS

To use a rotary cutter to its greatest advantage, first cut a strip of fabric, then subcut the strip into specific sizes. For example, if your instructions say to cut forty 2" squares, follow these steps.

1. First cut a 2"-wide strip crosswise on the fabric. Assuming you have squared up the fabric edge as described earlier, you can turn your cutting mat clockwise 180° with the newly squared-up edge on your left and the excess fabric on the right. Place the ruler on top of the fabric.

2. Align the 2" grid mark on the ruler with the squared-up edge of the fabric (see Photo 2). *Note:* Align only the vertical grid mark and the fabric raw edge; ignore the selvages at the lower edge that may not line up perfectly with the horizontal ruler grid. A good rule of thumb to remember when rotary-cutting fabric is "the piece you want to keep should be under the ruler." That way, if you accidentally swerve away from the ruler when cutting, the piece under the ruler will be "safe."

3. Placing your rotary cutter along the ruler's right-hand edge and holding the ruler firmly with your left hand, run the blade along the ruler, as in Step 3 of Squaring Up the Fabric Edge, *left,* to cut the strip. Remove the ruler.

4. Sliding the excess fabric out of the way, carefully turn the 2" strip so it is horizontal on the mat. Refer to Squaring Up the Fabric Edge to trim off the selvage edges, squaring up those fabric ends.

5. Then align the 2" grid mark on the ruler with the squared-up edge of the fabric (the 2" square you want to keep is under the ruler). Hold the

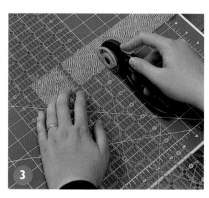

ruler with your left hand and run the rotary cutter along the right-hand ruler edge to cut a 2" square. You can cut multiple 2" squares from one strip by sliding the ruler over 2" from the previous cutting line and cutting again (see Photo 3). From a 44/45" strip, you'll likely be able to cut twenty-one 2" squares. Since in this example you need a total of 40, cut a second 2"-wide strip and subcut it into 2" squares.

CUTTING TRIANGLES

Right triangles also can be quickly and accurately cut with a rotary cutter. There are two common ways to cut triangles. An example of each method follows.

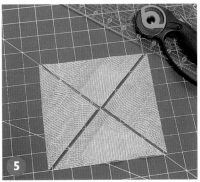

To cut two triangles from one square, the instructions may read:

From green print, cut:
- 20—3" squares, cutting each in half diagonally for a total of 40 triangles

1. Referring to Cutting and Subcutting Strips, on *page 152,* cut a 3"-wide fabric strip and subcut the strip into 3" squares.

2. Line up the ruler's edge with opposite corners of a square to cut it in half diagonally (see Photo 4). Cut along the ruler's edge. *Note:* The triangles' resultant long edges are on the bias. Avoid stretching or overhandling these edges when piecing so that seams don't become wavy and distorted.

To cut four triangles from one square, the instructions may read:

From green print, cut:
- 20—6" squares, cutting each diagonally twice in an X for a total of 80 triangles

3. Referring to Cutting and Subcutting Strips on *page 152,* cut a 6"-wide fabric strip and subcut it into 6" squares.

4. Line up the ruler's edge with opposite corners of a square to cut it in half diagonally. Cut along the ruler's edge; do not separate the two triangles created. Line up the ruler's edge with the remaining corners and cut to make a total of four triangles (see Photo 5). *Note:* The triangles' resultant short edges are on the bias. Avoid stretching or overhandling these edges when piecing so that seams don't become wavy and distorted.

CUTTING WITH TEMPLATES

A successful quilt requires precise cutting of pieces.

About Scissors

Sharp scissor blades are vital to accurate cutting, but keeping them sharp is difficult because each use dulls the metal slightly. Cutting paper and plastic speeds the dulling process, so invest in a second pair for those materials and reserve your best scissors for fabric.

Make the Templates

For some quilts, you'll need to cut out the same shape multiple times. For accurate piecing later, the individual pieces should be identical to one another.

A template is a pattern made from extra-sturdy material so you can trace around it many times without wearing away the edges. You can make your own templates by duplicating printed patterns (like those on the Pattern Sheets) on plastic.

To make permanent templates, we recommend using easy-to-cut template plastic. This material lasts indefinitely, and its transparency allows you to trace the pattern directly onto its surface.

To make a template, lay the plastic over a printed pattern. Trace the pattern onto the plastic using a ruler and a permanent marker. This will ensure straight lines, accurate corners, and permanency. *Note:* If the pattern you are tracing is a half-pattern to begin with, you must first make a full-size pattern. To do so, fold a piece of tracing paper in half and crease; unfold. Lay the tracing paper over the half-pattern, aligning the crease with the fold line indicated on the pattern. Trace the half pattern. Then rotate the tracing paper, aligning the half pattern on the opposite side of the crease to trace the other half of the pattern. Use this full-size pattern to create your template.

For hand piecing and appliqué, make templates the exact size of the finished pieces, without seam allowances, by tracing the patterns' dashed lines. For machine piecing, make templates with the seam allowances included.

For easy reference, mark each template with its letter designation, grain line if noted, and block name. Verify the template's size by placing it over the printed pattern. Templates must be accurate or the error, however small, will compound many times as you assemble the quilt. To check the accuracy of your templates, make a test block before cutting the fabric pieces for an entire quilt.

continued

Trace the Templates

To mark on fabric, use a special quilt marker that makes a thin, accurate line. Do not use a ballpoint or ink pen that may bleed if washed. Test all marking tools on a fabric scrap before using them.

To trace pieces that will be used for hand piecing or appliqué, place templates facedown on the wrong side of the fabric and trace; position the tracings at least ½" apart (see Diagram 1, Template A). The lines drawn on the fabric are the sewing lines. Mark cutting lines, or estimate by eye a seam allowance around each piece as you cut out the pieces. For hand piecing, add a ¼" seam allowance when cutting out the pieces; for hand appliqué, add a ³⁄₁₆" seam allowance.

Diagram 1

Templates used to make pieces for machine piecing have seam allowances included so you can use common lines for efficient cutting. Place templates facedown on the wrong side of the fabric and trace;

position them without space in between (see Diagram 2, Template B). Using sharp scissors or a rotary cutter and ruler, cut precisely on the drawn (cutting) lines.

Diagram 2

Templates for Angled Pieces

When two patchwork pieces come together and form an angled opening, a third piece must be set into this angle. This happens frequently when using diamond shapes.

For a design that requires setting in, a pinhole or window template makes it easy to mark the fabric with each shape's exact sewing and cutting lines and the exact point of each corner on the sewing line. By matching the corners of adjacent pieces, you'll be able to sew them together easily and accurately.

To make a pinhole template, lay template plastic over a pattern piece. Trace both the cutting and sewing lines onto the plastic. Carefully cut out the template on the cutting line. Using a sewing-machine needle or any large needle, make a hole in the

template at each corner on the sewing line (matching points). The holes must be large enough for a pencil point or other fabric marker to poke through.

Trace Angled Pieces

To mark fabric using a pinhole template, lay it facedown on the wrong side of the fabric and trace. Using a pencil, mark dots on the fabric through the holes in the template to create matching points. Cut out the fabric piece on the drawn line, making sure the matching points are marked.

To mark fabric using a window template, lay it facedown on the wrong side of the fabric (see Diagram 3). With a marking tool, mark the cutting line, sewing line, and each corner on the sewing line (matching points). Cut out the fabric piece on the cutting lines, making sure all pieces have sewing lines and matching points marked.

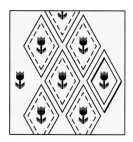

Diagram 3

PIECING

Patchwork piecing consists of sewing fabric pieces together in a specific pattern.

Hand Piecing

In hand piecing, seams are sewn only on the marked sewing lines rather than from one raw edge to the other. Begin by matching the edges of two pieces with the right sides of the fabrics together. Sewing lines should be marked on the wrong side of both pieces. Push a pin through both fabric

layers at each corner (see Diagram 1). Secure the pins perpendicular to the sewing line. Insert more pins between the corners.

Insert a needle through both fabrics at the seam-line corner. Make one or two backstitches atop the first stitch to secure the thread. Weave the needle in and out of the fabric along the seam line, taking four to six tiny

stitches at a time before you pull the thread taut (see Diagram 2). Remove the pins as you sew. Turn the work over occasionally to see that the stitching follows the marked sewing line on the other side.

Sew eight to 10 stitches per inch along the seam line. At the end of the seam, remove the last pin and make the ending stitch through the hole left

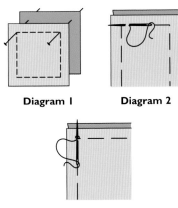

Diagram 1   **Diagram 2**

Diagram 3

by the corner pin. Backstitch over the last stitch and end the seam with a loop knot (see Diagram 3).

To join rows of patchwork by hand, hold the sewn pieces with right sides together and seams matching. Insert pins at corners of the matching pieces. Add additional pins as necessary, securing each pin perpendicular to the sewing line (see Diagram 4).

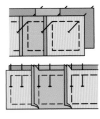

Diagram 4

Stitch the joining seam as before, but do not sew across the seam allowances that join the patches. At each seam allowance, make a backstitch or loop knot, then slide the needle through the seam allowance. (see Diagram 5). Knot or backstitch again to give the intersection strength, then sew the remainder of the seam. Press each seam as it is completed.

Diagram 5

Machine Piecing

Machine piecing depends on sewing an exact ¼" seam allowance. Some machines have a presser foot that is the proper width, or a ¼" foot is available. To check the width of a machine's presser foot, sew a sample seam, with the raw fabric edges aligned with the right edge of the presser foot; measure the resultant seam allowance using graph paper with a ¼" grid.

Using two different thread colors—one on top of the machine and one in the bobbin—can help you to better match your thread color to your fabrics. If your quilt has many fabrics, use a neutral color, such as gray or beige, for both the top and bobbin threads throughout the quilt.

Press for Success

In quilting, almost every seam needs to be pressed before the piece is sewn to another, so keep your iron and ironing board near your sewing area. It's important to remember to press with an up and down motion. Moving the iron around on the fabric can distort seams, especially those sewn on the bias.

Project instructions in this book generally tell you in what direction to press each seam. When in doubt, press both seam allowances toward the darker fabric. When joining rows of blocks, alternate the direction the seam allowances are pressed to ensure flat corners.

Setting in Pieces

The key to sewing angled pieces together is aligning marked matching points carefully. Whether you're stitching by machine or hand, start and stop sewing precisely at the matching points (see the dots in Diagram 6, top) and backstitch to secure the ends of the seams. This prepares the angle for the next piece to be set in.

Join two diamond pieces, sewing between matching points to make an angled unit (see Diagram 6).

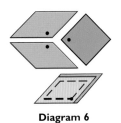

Diagram 6

Follow the specific instructions for either machine or hand piecing to complete the set-in seam.

MACHINE PIECING

With right sides together, pin one piece of the angled unit to one edge of the square (see Diagram 7). Match the seam's matching points by pushing a pin through both fabric layers to check the alignment. Machine-stitch the seam between the matching points. Backstitch to secure the ends of the seam; do not stitch into the ¼" seam allowance. Remove the unit from the sewing machine.

Bring the adjacent edge of the angled unit up and align it with the next edge of the square (see Diagram 8). Insert a pin in each corner to align matching points, then pin the remainder of the seam. Machine-stitch between matching points as before. Press the seam allowances of the set-in piece away from it.

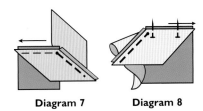

Diagram 7   **Diagram 8**

HAND PIECING

Pin one piece of the angled unit to one edge of the square with right sides together (see Diagram 9). Use pins to align matching points at the corners.

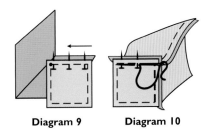

Diagram 9   **Diagram 10**

Hand-sew the seam from the open end of the angle into the corner. Remove pins as you sew between matching points. Backstitch at the corner to secure stitches. Do not sew into the ¼" seam allowance and do not cut your thread.

continued

Bring the adjacent edge of the square up and align it with the other edge of the angled unit. Insert a pin in each corner to align matching points, then pin the remainder of the seam (see Diagram 10 on *page 155*). Hand-sew the seam from the corner to the open end of the angle, removing pins as you sew. Press the seam allowances of the set-in piece away from it.

Mitered Border Corners

A border surrounds the piecework of many quilts. Angled, mitered corners add to a border's framed effect.

To add a border with mitered corners, first pin a border strip to a quilt top edge, matching the center of the strip and the center of the quilt top edge. Sew together, beginning and ending the seam ¼" from the quilt top corners (see Diagram 11). Allow excess border fabric to extend beyond the edges. Repeat with remaining border strips. Press

the seam allowances toward the border strips.

Overlap the border strips at each corner (see Diagram 12). Align the edge of a 90° right triangle with the raw edge of a top border strip so the long edge of the triangle intersects the seam in the corner. With a pencil, draw along the edge of the triangle from the border seam out to the raw edge. Place the bottom border strip on top and repeat the marking process.

With the right sides of adjacent border strips together, match the marked seam lines and pin (see Diagram 13).

Beginning with a backstitch at the inside corner, stitch exactly on the marked lines to the outside edges of the border strips. Check the right side of the corner to see that it lies flat. Then trim the excess fabric, leaving a ¼" seam allowance. Press the seam open. Mark and sew the remaining corners in this manner.

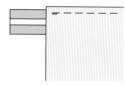

Diagram 11

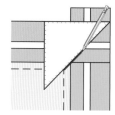

Diagram 12

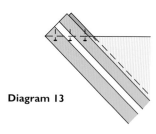

Diagram 13

APPLIQUÉ

With appliqué, you create a picture by stitching fabric shapes atop a foundation block.

Start Simple

We encourage beginners to select an appliqué design with straight lines and gentle curves. Learning to make sharp points and tiny stitches takes practice.

In the following instructions, we've used a stemmed flower motif as the appliqué example.

Baste the Seam Allowances

Begin by turning under the appliqué piece ³⁄₁₆" seam allowances; press. Some quilters like to thread-baste the folded edges to ensure proper placement. Edges that will be covered by other pieces don't need to be turned under.

For sharp points on tips, trim the seam allowance to within ⅛" of the

stitching line (see Photo 1 *opposite*); taper the sides gradually to ³⁄₁₆". Fold under the seam allowance remaining on the tips. Then turn the seam allowances under on both sides of the tips. The side seam allowances will overlap slightly at the tips, forming sharp points. Baste the folded edges in place (see Photo 2 *opposite*). The turned seam allowances may form little pleats on the back side that you also should baste in place. You'll remove the basting stitches after the shape has been appliquéd to the foundation.

Make Bias Stems

In order to curve gracefully, appliqué stems are cut on the bias. The strips for stems can be prepared in two ways. You can fold and press the

strip in thirds as shown in Photo 3 *opposite*. Or you can fold the bias strip in half lengthwise with the wrong side inside; press. Stitch ¼" in from the raw edges to keep them aligned. Fold the strip in half again, hiding the raw edges behind the first folded edge; press.

Position and Stitch

Pin the prepared appliqué pieces in place on the foundation using the position markings or referring to the block assembly diagram (see Photo 4 *opposite*). If your pattern suggests it, mark the position for each piece on the foundation block before you begin. Overlap the flowers and stems as indicated.

Using thread in colors that match the fabrics, sew each stem and blossom onto the foundation with small slip stitches as shown in Photo 5. (For photographic purposes, the thread color does not match the lily.)

Catch only a few threads of the stem or flower fold with each stitch. Pull the stitches taut but not so tight that they pucker the fabric. You can use the needle's point to manipulate the appliqué edges as needed. Take an extra slip stitch at the point of a petal to secure it to the foundation.

You can use hand-quilting needles for appliqué stitching, but some quilters prefer a longer milliner's or straw needle. The extra needle length aids in tucking fabric under before taking slip stitches.

If the foundation fabric shows through the appliqué fabrics, cut away the foundation fabric. Trimming the foundation fabric also reduces the bulk of multiple layers when quilting. Carefully trim the underlying fabric to within ¼" of the appliqué stitches (see Photo 6). Do not cut the appliqué fabric.

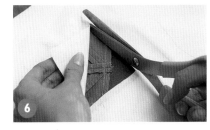
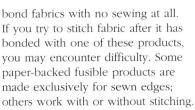

Fusible Appliqué

For quick-finish appliqué, use paper-backed fusible web. Then you can iron the shapes onto the foundation and add decorative stitching to the edges. This product consists of two layers, a fusible webbing lightly bonded to paper that peels off. The webbing adds a slight stiffness to the back of the appliqué pieces.

When you purchase this product, read the directions on the bolt end or packaging to make sure you're buying the right kind for your project. Some brands are specifically engineered to

bond fabrics with no sewing at all. If you try to stitch fabric after it has bonded with one of these products, you may encounter difficulty. Some paper-backed fusible products are made exclusively for sewn edges; others work with or without stitching.

If you buy paper-backed fusible web from a bolt, be sure fusing instructions are included because the iron temperature and timing varies by brand. This information is usually on the paper backing.

With any of these products, the general procedure is to trace the pattern wrong side up onto the paper

side of the fusible web. Then place the fusible web on the wrong side of the appliqué fabrics, paper side up, and use an iron to fuse the layers together. Then cut out the shapes, peel off the paper, turn the fabrics right side up, and fuse the shapes to the foundation fabric.

You also can fuse the fusible web and fabric together before tracing. You'll still need to trace templates wrong side up on the paper backing.

If you've used a no-sew fusible web, your appliqué is done. If not, finish the edges with hand or machine stitching.

CUTTING BIAS STRIPS

Strips for curved appliqué pattern pieces, such as meandering vines, and for binding curved edges should be cut on the bias (diagonally across the grain of a woven fabric), which runs at a 45° angle to the selvage and has the most give or stretch.

To cut bias strips, begin with a fabric square or rectangle. Use a large

acrylic ruler to square up the left edge of the fabric. Make the first cut at a 45° angle to the left edge (see Bias Strip Diagram). Handle the diagonal edges carefully to avoid distorting the bias. To cut a strip, measure the desired width parallel to the 45° cut edge; cut. Continue cutting enough strips to total the length needed.

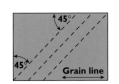

Bias Strip Diagram

COVERED CORDING

Finish pillows and quilts with easy, tailored cording.

Covered cording is made by sewing a bias-cut fabric strip around a length of cording. The width of the bias strip will vary depending on the diameter of your cording. Refer to the specific project instructions for those measurements. Regardless, the method used to cover the cording is the same.

With the wrong side inside, fold under 1½" at one end of the bias strip. With the wrong side inside, fold the strip in half lengthwise to make the cording cover. Insert the cording next to the folded edge, placing a cording end 1" from the cording cover folded end. Using a machine cording foot, sew through both fabric layers right next to the cording (see Diagram 1).

When attaching the cording to your project, begin stitching 1½" from the covered cording's folded end. Round the corners slightly, making sure the corner curves match. As you stitch each corner, gently ease the covered cording into place (see Diagram 2).

After going around the entire edge of the project, cut the end of the cording so that it will fit snugly into the folded opening at the beginning (see Diagram 3). The ends of the cording should abut inside the covering. Stitch the ends in place to secure (see Diagram 4).

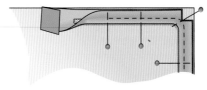

Diagram 2

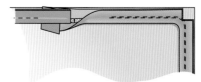

Diagram 3

Diagram 4

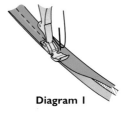

Diagram 1

HANGING SLEEVES

When you want a favorite quilt to become wall art,

hang it with care to avoid sagging, tearing, and wavy edges.

Quilts make wonderful pieces of wall art. When treated as museum pieces and hung properly, they won't deteriorate. Let size be your guide when determining how to hang your quilt.

Hang smaller quilts, a 25" square or less, with purchased clips, sewn-on tabs, or pins applied to the corners. Larger quilts require a hanging sleeve attached to the back. It may take a few minutes more to sew on a sleeve, but the effort preserves your hours of work with less distortion and damage.

Make a Hanging Sleeve

1. Measure the quilt's top edge.

2. Cut a 6"- to 10"-wide strip of prewashed fabric 2" longer than the quilt's top edge. For example, if the top edge is 40", cut a 6×42" strip. A 6"-wide strip is sufficient for a dowel or drapery rod. If you're using something bigger in diameter, cut a wider fabric strip. If you're sending your quilt to be displayed at a quilt show, adjust your

Diagram 1

Diagram 2

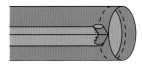

Diagram 3

measurements to accommodate the show's requirements.

3. Fold under 1½" on both short ends of the fabric strip. Sew ¼" from raw edges (see Diagram 1).

4. Fold the fabric strip in half lengthwise with the wrong side inside; pin. Stitch together the long edges with a ¼" seam allowance (see Diagram 2) to make the sleeve. Press

the seam allowance open and center the seam in the middle of the sleeve (see Diagram 3).

5. Center the sleeve on the quilt backing about 1" below the binding with the seam facing the backing (see Diagram 4). Stitching through the backing and batting, slip-stitch the sleeve to the quilt along both long edges and the portions of the short edges that touch the backing.

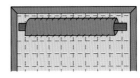

Diagram 4

6. Slide a wooden dowel or slender piece of wood that is 1" longer than the finished sleeve into the sleeve and hang as desired.

FINISHING

The final step in quiltmaking is to bind the edges.

Layering

Cut and piece the backing fabric to measure at least 3" bigger on all sides than the quilt top. Press all seam allowances open. with wrong sides together, layer the quilt top and backing fabric with the batting in between; baste. Quilt as desired.

Binding

The binding for most quilts is cut on the straight grain of the fabric. If your quilt has curved edges, cut the strips on the bias (see *page 157*). The cutting instructions for projects in this book specify the number of binding strips or a total length needed to finish the quilt. The instructions also specify enough width for a French-fold or double-layer binding because it's easier to apply and adds durability.

Join the strips with diagonal seams to make one continuous binding strip

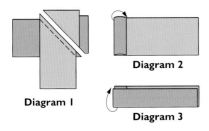

Diagram 1

Diagram 2

Diagram 3

(see Diagram 1). Trim the excess fabric, leaving ¼" seam allowances. Press the seam allowances open. Then, with the wrong sides together, fold under 1" at one end of the binding strip (see Diagram 2); press. Fold the strip in half lengthwise (see Diagram 3); press.

Beginning in the center of one side, place the binding strip against the right side of the quilt top, aligning the binding strip's raw edges with the quilt top's raw edge (see Diagram 4). Beginning 1½" from the folded edge, sew through all layers, stopping ¼" from the corner. Backstitch, then clip the threads. Remove the quilt from under the sewing-machine presser foot.

Fold the binding strip upward (see Diagram 5), creating a diagonal fold, and finger-press.

Holding the diagonal fold in place with your finger, bring the binding strip down in line with the next edge, making a horizontal fold that aligns with the top edge of the quilt (see Diagram 6).

Start sewing again at the top of the horizontal fold, stitching through all layers. Sew around the quilt, turning each corner in the same manner.

When you return to the starting point, lap the binding strip inside the beginning fold (see Diagram 7).

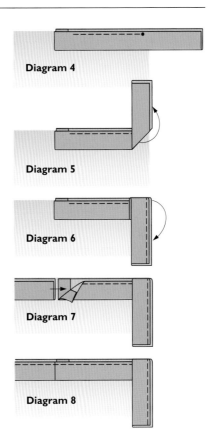

Diagram 4

Diagram 5

Diagram 6

Diagram 7

Diagram 8

Finish sewing to the starting point (see Diagram 8). Trim the batting and backing fabric even with the quilt top edges.

Turn the binding over the edge of the quilt to the back. Hand-stitch the binding to the backing fabric, making sure to cover any machine stitching.

To make mitered corners on the back, hand-stitch the binding up to a corner; fold a miter in the binding. Take a stitch or two in the fold to secure it. Then stitch the binding in place up to the next corner. Finish each corner in the same manner.

CREDITS

Quilt Designers

Cindy Blackberg
Railroad Crossing
A student of turn-of-the-century quilts, designer Cindy Blackberg combines designs and colors from that era with today's tools and techniques to create intricate heirlooms.

Sandy Bonsib
Something to Crow About
Folk art and memory quilts are designer Sandy Bonsib's specialty. Besides designing quilts, she teaches and is the author of several quilting books.

Kim Diehl
Pinwheels & Posies
A self-taught quilter, Kim Diehl designs quilts with homespun charm. Her foray into teaching has given her new insights on different ways to achieve quilting success.

Sarah Rhodes Dillow
Triangles in a Triangle
Curator and quilt historian Sarah Rhodes Dillow shares her love of vintage quilts by re-creating them with today's textiles.

Becky Goldsmith and Linda Jenkins
Butterfly Garden
Pattern designers Linda Jenkins, *far left*, and Becky Goldsmith of Piece O' Cake Designs develop methods for accomplishing challenging quilting tasks, such as perfect appliqué placement.

Sharlene Jorgensen
Apple Core
Inspired by everyday objects, such as wallpaper and floor tiles, as well as unusual or intriguing items, designer Sharlene Jorgensen was among the first to use a computer to help her develop quilt designs.

Jill Kemp
Under the Stars
Designer Jill Kemp shares her love of the country through her quilts. She looks to nature, taking inspiration from familiar shapes and natural colors to add folk art flavor to timeless designs.

Betty Lenz
Scrap Apple
Designer Betty Lenz enjoys combining challenging quilt techniques, here foundation piecing and needle-turn appliqué, to create quilts with widespread appeal.

Stephanie Martin Glennon
Noah's Garden
When she quilts, designer Stephanie Martin Glennon relies on nature and ordinary joys for her inspiration. Her childlike delight in life is evident in her cheerful creations.

Jill Abeloe Mead
Razzle Dazzle
Quilting is a family affair for designer Jill Abeloe Mead as her quilt projects often showcase the fabrics designed by her son, Peter Mead. Jill's unique garment designs are available through her company, Rag Merchant.

Jan Wildman
Spring Leaves
Traditional piecing and free-motion machine quilting are designer Jan Wildman's forte. She teaches free-motion quilting, where she encourages her students to add exciting, attractive designs to their quilts.

Darlene Zimmerman
Hugs and Kisses
Quilt designer and teacher Darlene Zimmerman takes inspiration from antique quilts, vintage fabrics, and collectibles. She designs fabrics and quilting tools, and is the author of several books and articles on quilting.

Laura Boehnke
Quilt Tester
With her keen color sense and astute use of fabrics, quilt tester Laura Boehnke gives each project an entirely different look as she verifies the pattern, something she's been doing for *American Patchwork & Quilting* magazine since its inception.

Project Quilters and Finishers
Janet Brandt
Kate Hardy
Cindy Maruth
Deb Mulder
Heather Mulder
Mabeth Oxenreider
Janelle Swenson
Sue Urich

Materials Suppliers
Chanteclaire
Hoffman Fabrics
Lands' End
Marcus Brothers Textiles
Mission Valley Textiles
Moda
Northcott/Monarch
P&B Textiles
RJR Fashion Fabrics
Robert Kaufman Fine Fabrics
Timeless Treasures

Photographers
Craig Anderson: pages 22, 46, 57, 62, 65, 77, 78, 85, 101, 102, 103, 116, 117, 119, 129, 138, and 149
Marcia Cameron: pages 12, 14, 16, 32, 36, 55, 82, 118, and 127
Hopkins Associates: pages 19, 105, and 108
Scott Little: pages 13, 59, 76, 91, 109, 128, 130, and 131
Perry Struse: pages 8, 15, 17, 21, 23, 25, 26, 28, 33, 37, 41, 45, 47, 48, 54, 56, 60, 63, 64, 69, 74, 83, 84, 87, 96, 110, 111, 112, 115, 122, 125, 133, 141, 142, 147, and 149
Steve Struse: pages 10, 42, 72, 73, 80, 89, 98, 134, and 145